CHARLES BRENTON FISK
Organ Builder

VOLUME II

CHARLES BRENTON FISK
Organ Builder

VOLUME TWO
HIS WORK

COMPILED & EDITED
BY BARBARA OWEN

The Westfield Center for Early Keyboard Studies
Easthampton Massachusetts
1 9 8 6

Designed by Carol J. Blinn at Warwick Press, Easthampton, Massachusetts
Printed by The Studley Press of Dalton, Massachusetts

© 1986 by The Westfield Center for Early Keyboard Studies, Inc.

The following articles appear with kind permission:
"The Architect as Organ Maker"
reprinted from *Faith and Form*
Journal of the Interfaith Forum on Religion, Art and Architecture

"The Organ's Breath of Life"
© *The Diapason*

"*Pipe Flueways*"
© 1975 The American Guild of Organists
reprinted from *Music: The AGO/RCCO Magazine*

"Some Thoughts on Pipe Metal"
© 1978 The American Guild of Organists
reprinted from *Music: The AGO/RCCO Magazine*

"How Certain Musical Differences..."
© McGill University
reprinted from *L'Orgue à notre Époque*

Manufactured in the United States of America

ISBN 0-9616755-0-0
VOLUME II   ISBN 0-9616755-2-7

Frontispiece: Charles Fisk at the organ at Wellesley College
CREDIT: Paul Foley

TABLE OF CONTENTS

Preface

THE LEGACY OF CHARLES FISK

- 1 The Organs: 1956-84
- 77 List of Organs
- 83 Photographs, Sketches, and Diagrams

WRITINGS OF CHARLES FISK

PUBLISHED ARTICLES

- 109 The Architect as Organ Maker
- 113 The Organ's Breath of Life
- 121 Pipe Flueways
- 123 Some Thoughts on Pipe Metal
- 127 How Certain Musical Differences between the Historic Organs of Germany and France were Achieved by Differences in Construction

UNPUBLISHED ARTICLES AND TALKS

- 135 The Spanish Baroque Organ in Mexico Cathedral
- 139 Articulateness and the Organ: A Problem for the Organ Builder
- 145 In Memory of Carl Theodore Young
- 149 Singular Aspects of the Organ Reform in America

A CHARLES FISK MISCELLANY

- 153 Greensboro College Organ and Church Music Conference, 1980
- 163 Excerpts from Letters
- 177 Excerpts from the European Notebooks
- 189 Poem: "Sea Mossing at Milk Island"

191 Discography
195 Bibliography

PREFACE

Organ builders as a group tend toward record longevity; by this yardstick Charles Brenton Fisk (1925–1983) died before his time. Of his 58 years among us, 33 were spent in learning and practicing the craft of organ building, 25 of these as President and sole owner of the company known as C. B. Fisk, Inc. During this quarter century of creative activity, Charles Fisk was responsible for the design, voicing, and building of 45 new organs, the rebuilding and restoration of a handful of others, and the preliminary design of two or three instruments which he did not live to see completed.

In terms of actual volume, Charles Fisk's output as an organ builder was not great; some larger firms are capable of producing 45 organs in a year or two of work. In terms of influence, however, the work and thought of Charles Fisk have had an incalculable impact on the direction which American organ building has taken in the second half of the twentieth century. Because they were the product of a mind that was continuously learning, questioning, and growing, there is surprising variety among these instruments. If there is any unifying characteristic at all, it is a carefully calculated eclecticism. Charles Fisk acknowledged what many could not accept in the 1950s—if an organ is to be really good, if it is to soar above mere functionalism and be a work of art, it simply cannot be all things to all people. But he also believed that if an organ was truly well-designed and beautifully voiced, if it brought music of any kind to life on a high level, then it would always be capable of more than it might appear to be able to do.

Over and over again, the instruments which Charles Fisk built have proven the validity of his concepts. He drew his material from historic sources, he listened to other peoples' ideas, and, perhaps most important of all, he listened to music. But he used what he learned in a way which was uniquely his own, and every instrument he built bears the thumb-print of his individuality, and of the eclecticism of his taste.

This volume is a record of the life-work of Charles Fisk. It falls, essentially, into two parts. The first deals with the instruments which he built, recording, wherever possible, his own thoughts and commentary on them. The second is a compilation of his writings, both published and unpublished. Charles Fisk was a good writer, able to put his philosophies and insights into words in a readable, cogent fashion. We have felt that his memory would be best served, and the understanding of his work best furthered, not as much by writing about him as by allowing him to speak for himself.

Many people have assisted in the preparation of this volume, without whose contributions it would have been much less complete. Special thanks are due to the staff of C. B. Fisk, Inc., Gloucester, Massachusetts, for all their assistance and encouragement, and particularly to Virginia Lee Fisk, Robert Cornell, and Stephen Dieck. Thanks are due also to Lynn Edwards and Edward Pepe, as well as editorial advisor Deborah Robson, for their constructive comments on the format and manuscript.

BARBARA OWEN
Newburyport, Massachusetts
February, 1986

THE LEGACY OF CHARLES FISK

The Organs: 1956–84

> I have found that, for myself and for my own work, it matters very little what my detractors say about me. I think of myself as having a very specific job to do, namely, to find out the truth about what has made the organ a glorious instrument, and to pass on, by example, as much of that truth as I can in the time allotted me.
>
> Charles Fisk to Bryan Gerlach, July 27, 1982

THE PURPOSE OF THIS VOLUME is not to provide a biography of Charles Fisk, but to survey his contribution to the art of organ building and to record his own insights into his work. Because some biographical background is always helpful in understanding a man and his work, however, Fisk's own biographical account—written in 1972 to accompany an application for a Guggenheim Fellowship (which he did not get)—provides a fitting introduction:

> Although I have been actively interested in music all my life, my initial field of endeavor was physics, conditioned by work at Los Alamos, New Mexico, during World War II. After the war I majored in Physics at Harvard University (A.B., 1949) and worked subsequently in Cosmic Ray research at the Brookhaven Laboratory. In 1950 I resumed formal studies at the Graduate School of Physics, Stanford University, but shortly thereafter transferred to the Graduate School of Music in the same institution, having at last realized that my chief interest was unquestionably music, and that my chief contribution must of necessity combine physics and music. I apprenticed then to an organ builder near Stanford [John Swinford] and simultaneously studied early performance practice under Prof. Putnam Aldrich and George Houle. . . . After three years I went to work for the most avant garde American organ builder of the time, Walter Holtkamp, Sr.; thence after two years into partnership (1955) with a progressive young organ builder in Massachusetts [Thomas W. Byers] who three years later sold his interest to me, thus making me the proprietor of an organ building business [Andover Organ Company]. In 1961 I moved this business from Methuen to Gloucester, Massachusetts, under the name of C. B. Fisk, Inc. Because I have not wanted to lose control of the quality or character of the work, I have purposely kept the size of the firm small, i.e., we have never employed more than ten persons at one time.

During the decade after this statement was made, the size of the firm did grow to slightly exceed ten people, and the company moved from its original ramshackle former ropewalk to a more spacious new building in a Gloucester industrial park. But while Fisk was able to surround himself with exceptionally gifted men and women—who now continue his tradition of excellence and creativity—he remained the ultimate arbiter of the visual and tonal design of all Fisk organs to the end of his life.

Appended to this section is a complete list of the work of the Fisk firm from 1956 (Opus 24) to 1986. The numbering system used by the Fisk firm for its organs has been a cause of some confusion. It was begun by Thomas Byers, who founded the original Andover Organ Company in 1949, and continued by Fisk both after he purchased Byers's interest in the firm in 1958, and after he changed the name of the firm to C. B. Fisk, Inc. in 1961. With the exception of a small unit organ, built by Byers in 1953, all numbers from 1 through 24 refer to jobs in which an older organ was rebuilt or added to. After 1961 certain of Fisk's employees who did not wish to move to Gloucester remained in Methuen and formed a new company using the old Andover name. To this new firm Charles Fisk, wishing to concentrate on new organs, turned over six contracts for rebuilding older organs already in hand—numbers 32, 38, 39, 40, 41, and 43. While most of Fisk's work following Opus 35 consisted of new instruments, a few major rebuilding and restoration projects did receive numbers: 36, 53, 61, and 73 (the last-named subcontracted to A. David Moore). Other such projects, ranging from minor alterations to full-fledged rebuilds and restorations, were eventually given special "J" numbers. Finally, a few gaps occur on the list due to cancelled contracts: 58, 60, 63, and 80.

The first projects in which Charles Fisk was directly involved had already been contracted for by Byers. No. 24 was the rebuilding of an electric-action organ in the First Congregational Church of Williamstown, Massachusetts; No. 26, the enlargement of a tracker-action organ in the First Religious Society of Newburyport, Massachusetts; and No. 27, a similar job on a smaller scale for the First Unitarian Church of Billerica, Massachusetts. These two last-named projects, completed in 1956 and 1957, gave Fisk valuable experience in working with mechanical action, and helped to confirm his commitment to this type of action. No. 30 was a five-rank unit organ incorporating many old parts which was installed in the chapel of the First Congregational Church of Cambridge, Massachusetts.

The first instrument built by Fisk and Byers which might be called a true "opus" was No. 25, built for the Chapel of Rice University in Houston, Texas. It was an entirely new organ, laid out in a manner faintly reminiscent of Holtkamp, with a neo-baroque specification. While it had slider windchests, its playing action was electro-pneumatic. Shortly before the completion of this organ Byers sold his interest in the company to Fisk, who from this time on was sole proprietor.

Opus 25, 1958
Rice University Chapel, Houston, Texas

Great (enclosed):		Positive:	
Spitzprincipal	8'	Gedacktflöte	8'
Lieblich Gedeckt	8'	Spitzflöte	4'
Octave	4'	Principal	2'
Rohrflöte	4'	Larigot	1⅓'
Tertian	II	Cimbel	II
Mixture	III–V		
Krummhorn	8'		
		Pedal:	
		Subbass	16'
		Octave	8'
		Gedeckt	8'
		(Quinte	5⅓')
		(Gedeckt	8')
		(Superoctave	4')

Couplers: Great/Pedal, Positive/Pedal, Positive/Great
Manual compass: 56 notes; Pedal compass: 32 notes
Wind pressure: Manuals, 2¼"; Pedal, 3"

The Rice instrument was the last completely electric-action organ to be built by Charles Fisk. All future organs were to have mechanical manual action, although for some years electric action was still used wholly or partly in pedal actions and, in larger instruments, for the drawstop and combination action.

Rebuilding work still claimed some of the job numbers in this period, but Opus 28, a small organ for Redeemer Lutheran Church in Lawrence, Massachusetts, has the distinction of being the first all-new instrument to be built under Fisk's sole direction. Completed in 1959, it had mechanical manual key action, and electro-pneumatic stop and pedal action.

Opus 28, 1959
Redeemer Lutheran Church, Lawrence, Massachusetts

Great:		Brustwerk:	
Hohlflote	8'	Spitzflote	8'
Praestant	4'	Rohrflote	4'
Terzian	II	Principal	2'
Scharf	II–IV		
	Pedal:		
	Gedecktbass	16'	
	(Gedeckt	8')	
	(Gedecktflote	4')	

Couplers: Great/Pedal, Brustwerk/Pedal, Brustwerk/Great
Manual compass: 56 notes; Pedal compass: 32 notes

In the same year, an ambitious specification was drawn up for Opus 31, a two-manual organ to be constructed for St. John's Episcopal Church, Westwood, Massachusetts. The plan was to build the Rückpositiv division first and to install it in the church's temporary sanctuary, completing the Great and pedal divisions after a new church was built. Financial problems ultimately forced changes in the church's plans, however. The temporary sanctuary was later remodeled into a permanent one and the Rückpositiv, originally standing on the main floor, was reinstalled in its proper position on the rear gallery rail, where it continues to serve as a one-manual organ (with a two-manual console).

Opus 31, 1959
St. John's Episcopal Church, Westwood, Massachusetts

Rückpositiv:		Pedal: (electric action)	
Gedeckt	8'	Bourdon	16'
Prestant	4'		
Spillflöte	4'		
Octave	2'		
Larigot	1⅓'		
Scharff	II–III		

Coupler: Rückpositiv/Pedal
Manual compass: 56 notes; Pedal compass: 32 notes

A backlog of work began to accumulate in this period, and several additional employees were hired. One of these was Fritz Noack, who left a few years later to form his own company. To Noack Fisk entrusted the execution of Opus 42, a small positive organ of three stops (Stopped Diapason 8', Chimney Flute 4', and Fifteenth 2') completed in 1960 for Daniel Pinkham of Cambridge.

Charles Fisk's first truly significant organ was Opus 35, a large two-manual instrument of classic design built for Mount Calvary Episcopal Church in Baltimore, Maryland. On its completion in 1961 Fisk moved his company to larger facilities in Gloucester, Massachusetts, and changed its name to C. B. Fisk, Inc. From this point onward, all individual organs will be discussed in detail. Wherever possible, Charles Fisk's own comments and observations on the instrument are included. These are drawn from a variety of sources—dedication programs, publicity releases, record jacket notes, letters—and it is hoped that they will offer some small glimpse of the thought and philosophy behind the individual instruments.

Opus 35, 1961
Mount Calvary Episcopal Church, Baltimore, Maryland

Hoovdwerk (Manual II):		Rugwerk (Manual I):	
Bourdon	16'	Holpijp	8'
Prestant	8'	Quintadeen	8'
Roerfluit	8'	Prestant	4'
Fluitdous	8'	Roerpijp	4'
Octaaf	4'	Nasard	2⅔'
Spitsfluit	4'	Octaaf	2'
Quint	2⅔'	Terts	1⅗'
Superoctaaf	2'	Quinta	1⅓'
Blokfluit	2'	Siffluit	1'
Mixtuur	IV	Scherp	III
Cymbaal	III	Krumhoorn	8'
Cornet	III		
Trompet	8' (en chamade)		

Pedaal:	
Subbas	16'
Lieflijk Gedekt	16'
Octaaf	8'
Gedektpommer	8'
Superoctaaf	4'
Vlakfluit	4'
Nachthoorn	2'
Ruispijp	IV
Mixtuur	IV
Fagot	16'
Trompet	8'
Schalmei	4'

Couplers: Rugwerk/Pedaal, Rugwerk/Hoovdwerk
Zymbelstern
Two combination pedals affecting Hoovdwerk only
Manual compass: 56 notes; Pedal compass: 32 notes
Wind pressures: Manuals, 1¾"; Pedal, 2⅜"

This organ was from the beginning intended to have at least thirty stops, the original plan calling for three manuals. In designing the instrument, Charles Fisk consulted extensively with Arthur Howes, organist of the church, and the Dutch organ builder Dirk A. Flentrop. During the summer of 1959 Fisk made his first trip to Europe, accompanied by Howes. Many facets of the organ design fell into place on this trip. Referring to discussions held with Flentrop, Fisk wrote:

> The signal decision arising out of our conferences was that of making for Mount Calvary a two-manual instead of a three-manual instrument. As you know, Arthur has all along been uncertain of which he would prefer; initially I had influenced him to decide upon three manuals, perhaps because, as we all know, there is a certain rakish snob-appeal attached to the third manual, especially among the laity. It was Dick Flentrop who resisted this idea quite strongly, however, on the grounds that the physical situation of the balcony will admit of a perfect two manual, but only of an imperfect three manual, organ.
>
> Charles Fisk to Rev. MacAllister Ellis, August 26, 1959

Also discarded were earlier ideas of making the stop action electro-pneumatic, and of providing combination pistons. This was to be a model organ, with no compromises. Fisk closed his letter to Ellis by stating "... I now have complete confidence that we can build an organ in the continental tradition which will surely live up to the highest ideals of that tradition."

Visually, Fisk took as his departure point the late Gothic organ-case in Amiens Cathedral, and draftsman Leo Constantineau worked up the details of the case design. By the end of the year work on the organ was under way, and Fisk discussed last-minute details with Howes:

> I think the Fluit Dous must be a kind of Dulciana, and at 8 foot. The mouths and taper are made different from those of the 4 foot flute mainly to avoid similarity, but although we use quarter mouths, the stop will be very soft—soft, but masculine.
>
> I still would rather not have the Great and Positive 8 foot flutes scaled the same. No matter what one does with chimneys, ears and mouths, they must sound somewhat similar if they are alike in scale; they must have the same weight in the chorus. I thoroughly agree that all four flutes must be of comparable intensity so that they can be used together, but I would give them each a different color and each a different amount of fundamental. It is our plan to use large chimneys on the Positive 4 foot flute, which will give it somewhat the quality of a Nachthorn. The Nazard will be quite large. And finally, we will do our best to make the chiff of the flutes controllable.

> As the jigsaw puzzle starts to go together in our minds, it begins to look as though we have conceived the right instrument for this situation. In nearly all directions we have managed to trim it down so that it should have a very reasonable form, without any grossness. Building by the old principles certainly has its merits; everything is so *reasonable*.
>
> Charles Fisk to Arthur Howes, December 30, 1959

The organ was completed in 1961 and dedicated in a series of recitals held October 16 through 19 played by Arthur Howes, Donald Mackey, Piet Kee, and Heinz Wunderlich. These were followed by a dedicatory service on October 20. As the tonal finishing of the organ was nearing completion, Charles Fisk wrote of it: "I think I can safely say that this organ *is* a work of art, and as far as I am concerned this is the thing above all things" (Charles Fisk to Hubert Lamb, July 17, 1961).

Opus 37, 1962
Jewett Arts Center, Wellesley College, Wellesley, Massachusetts

Great:		Brustwerk:	
Gedeckt	8'	Quintaton	8'
Principal	4'	Gemshorn	2'
Mixture	II		
		Pedal:	
		Bourdon	16'

Couplers: Great/Pedal, Brustwerk/Pedal, Brustwerk/Great
Manual compass: 56 notes; Pedal compass: 32 notes

This small instrument was built at the request of Melville Smith, then organ instructor at Wellesley College, who died suddenly just before the organ was to be installed. In a letter to Hubert Lamb dated July 16, 1962, Fisk wrote: "I am so terribly sorry that he [Smith] will not be able to use the only organ I was ever able to build for him." Smith was not only a strong supporter of Charles Fisk's work but one who had a significant influence on his musical tastes.

The visual and tonal design of the Wellesley organ reveal a kinship to the earlier Opus 28. It also became a prototype for seven other instruments built in substantially the same style in subsequent years. The first of these were:

BOSTON UNIVERSITY SCHOOL OF FINE ARTS, BOSTON: Opus 47, 1965
ST. PAUL'S CATHOLIC CHURCH, GREENCASTLE, INDIANA: Opus 48, 1965
DEPAUW UNIVERSITY, GREENCASTLE, INDIANA: Opus 48a, 1965

These three instruments differ from Opus 37 in having an additional stop (Sesquialtera I–II) on the Great, and an extended Pedal Bourdon mechanically duplexed at 16' and 8' pitches. The nomenclature differs slightly, the 8' and 4' stops on the Great being called Stopped Diapason and Prestant, the Brustwerk 8' called Quintadena. While the Bourdon 16', Gedeckt 8', and Quintaton 8' bass in Opus 37 are of wood, the corresponding stops in Opus 47, Opus 48, Opus 48a, and subsequent organs are of metal.

NORTH CAROLINA SCHOOL OF THE ARTS, WINSTON-SALEM, NORTH CAROLINA: Opus 59, 1969
FRANK TAYLOR RESIDENCE, NEWTON, MASSACHUSETTS: Opus 59a, 1970

Opus 59 is identical to 48 and 48a except that the Pedal rank was extended further to provide a 4' stop. Opus 59a was modified considerably by the addition of a Cromorne to the second manual, a Tremulant, and a 16' Basson (unified at 16', 8', and 4') to the Pedal. The stop action is electrical, and there is also a combination action. Although the stops are essentially the same as those in the other organs, the stop nomenclature is French, and is as follows:

Opus 59a, 1970
Frank Taylor Residence, Newton, Massachusetts

Positif:		Recit:	
Flute à Cheminée	8'	Bourdon	8'
Prestant	4'	Quarte de Nasard	2'
Cornet	I–II	Cromorne	8'
Fourniture	III		
		Pedal:	
		Bourdon	16'
		(Flûte	8')
		(Cor de Nuit	4')
		Basson	16'
		(Dulciane	8')
		(Musette	4')

This organ was moved to the chapel of St. Barnabas' Episcopal Church, Falmouth, Massachusetts, following the death of Frank Taylor in 1985.

DUKE UNIVERSITY, DURHAM, NORTH CAROLINA: Opus 77, 1978
ST. BARTHOLOMEW'S EPISCOPAL CHURCH, ATLANTA, GEORGIA: Opus 77a, 1978

These two organs are identical, and differ only slightly from the previous ones. The Pedal compass has been reduced from 32 to 30 notes, and the duplexing eliminated, leaving the Pedal with only a 16' stop as in the original Opus 37. In Manual I the Sesquialtera and Mixture have been made double-drawing, allowing separate use of their 2⅔' and 2' ranks.

Opus 77a was dedicated on April 14, 1978, with a recital by Charles Krigbaum.

Opus 44, 1964
King's Chapel, Boston, Massachusetts

Great:		Swell:	
Bourdon	16'	Violin Diapason	8'
Open Diapason	8' (I–II)	Stopt Diapason	8'
Spire Flute	8'	Dulciana	8'
Octave	4'	Principal	4'
Chimney Flute	4'	Rohrpipe	4'
Twelfth	2⅔'	Flageolet	2'
Fifteenth	2'	Sesquialtera	II
Seventeenth	1⅗'	Sharp	III
Mixture	IV–VI	Bassoon	16'
Trumpet	8'	Trumpet	8'
Clarion	4'	Shawm	4'

Choir:		Pedal:	
Stopt Diapason	8'	Open Bass	16'
Flute	4'	Echo Bourdon	16'
Fifteenth	2'	Octave	8'
Nazard	1⅓'	Flute	8'
Mixture	II–III	Twelfth	5⅓'
Vox Humana	16'	Fifteenth	4'
		Blockflute	2'
		Mixture	IV
		Trombone	16'
		Cornopean	8'

THE ORGANS: 1956-84

Couplers: Swell/Great, Choir/Great, Great/Pedal, Swell/Pedal, Choir/Pedal
Swell Tremulant, Choir Tremulant, Crescendo Pedal
Electric stop action with 4 General and 14 Divisional Combinations, Cancel, and Great to Pedal Reversible
Manual compass: 61 notes; Pedal compass: 32 notes
Wind pressure: 2⅛" (later raised to 2³⁄₁₆")

    A number of revoiced stops from the previous E. M. Skinner organ of 1909 were incorporated into this organ, including three mixtures and a Fifteenth which Fisk had placed in that organ in 1960. Nearly all of the Pedal stops contain old pipes, with the exception of the Mixture and Cornopean; the Trombone combines old resonators with new shallots, tongues, and boots. All other reed stops were new save for the 16' Vox Humana, reworked from an 8' stop of the same name. The Pedal Open Bass and all wood flutes contain old pipes, as do the strings, the Spire Flute (reworked from an old Erzahler), the 4' Principal in the Great, and the 8' and 4' Principals in the Swell.
    The organ stands in the gallery of a building devoid of reverberation, housed in a replica of the church's 1756 organ case which had housed the previous organ. Both of these factors presented challenges:

> A major design problem was how to dispose the new instrument according to the cabinet, or "werk" principle within an 18th century single case. This problem was solved by situating the organ case well forward in the gallery and letting two divisions speak toward the front, the other two to the backwall. This wall, being newly constructed of hard plaster, functions not only as an efficient reflector but gives to the rearward projected sound a quality which enables it to be distinguished from the sound emanating from the front of the case. The Choir and Great divisions are in the front of the case, the Choir directly over the keydesk (in "Brustwerk" position), the Great in its traditional place behind the facade with its 8' and 4' Principals in burnished tin in prospect. The Swell is located above and behind the Great. Separately controllable swell openings face both forward and backward. The Pedal is within the main case beneath the Swell and speaks primarily to the backwall.
>
> In anticipation of [the acoustical] problem unusually large scales were employed for the Pedal Bass pipes, and many reed stops of great harmonic development were included in the specification. The result is a clean but highly complex plenum sound in which every motion of the player at the keyboard is made apparent to the listener, and which, because of the ideal placement in the rear gallery, achieves a degree of diffusion which suggests to the listener a longer reverberation period than is actually present.
>
>   Charles Fisk in *The American Organist*, January 1965

A few years later, in response to a question about acoustics from a member of the church, Fisk wrote:

> When knowing people learned that we were to build an organ for King's Chapel, they were astonished that we would even attempt so difficult an acoustical problem, and they were yet more astonished when the organ turned out to be a musical success. The credit we have received for building this organ has been like the credit a blind man receives for prowess among his sighted competitors. Such a man would gladly trade all credit for the restoration of his sight.
> Charles Fisk to Robert F. Bradford, January 14, 1970

Despite the organ's success, certain stops in the organ caused Charles Fisk dissatisfaction over the years. Among them were the mixtures which he had placed in the old organ and reused in the new one, and the Great reeds, purchased from an Austrian firm, which from the beginning had been judged too thin and unblending. The Choir Mixture was modified only a few years after the completion of the organ, and in 1979 a new mixture of larger scale was provided in place of the Swell Sharp. A year later the Trumpet 8' and Clarion 4' of the Great were replaced by a larger-scale French-style Trumpet and an 8' Cromorne, both made in the Fisk pipe shop.

The King's Chapel organ—the first three-manual instrument with tracker action to be built by an American firm in the twentieth century—was dedicated on February 2, 1964, in a concert given by Leonard Raver, assisted by members of the New England Conservatory Orchestra. Included in the program was the premiere performance of Daniel Pinkham's *Concertante* for organ, brass, and percussion, the first movement of which is based on the notes C—B—F.

Opus 45, 1965
Christ Episcopal Church, Westerly, Rhode Island

Great:		Swell:	
Bourdon	16'	Geigen Principal	8'
Prestant	8'	Flute Douce	8'
Chimney Flute	8'	Flute Céleste (tenor C)	8'
Octave	4'	Spindle Flute	4'
Twelfth	2⅔'	Octave	2'
Fifteenth	2'	Sesquialtera	II
Seventeenth	1⅗'	Sharp	IV
Mixture	IV–VI	Cremona	8'
Trumpet (en chamade)	8'		
Clarion (en chamade)	4'		

Choir (Rückpositiv):		Pedal:	
Bourdon	8'	Principal	16'
Prestant	4'	Bourdon	16'
Rohrpipe	4'	Octave	8'
Nazard	2⅔'	Gedeckt	8'
Gemshorn	2'	Super Octave	4'
Fife	1'	Sesquialtera	II
Cymbel	II–III	Mixture	IV
		Bassoon	16'
		Trumpet	8'
		Clarion	4'

Couplers: Swell/Great, Choir/Great, Swell/Pedal, Great/Pedal, Choir/Pedal
Cimbelstern, Swell Tremulant, Crescendo Pedal
Electro-pneumatic stop action with 15 combinations, Cancel, and Great to Pedal Reversible
Compass: Great and Swell, 61 notes; Choir, 56 notes; Pedal, 32 notes

In this church Charles Fisk was again faced with factors which affected the design of the organ. Although a new balcony had been built for the organ and choir, the church mandated that a group of three stained-glass windows not be significantly obscured.

The solution chosen was to "bracket" the windows in such a way as to combine organ and windows into a single harmonious composition.

By good fortune, the particular configuration of the windows lends itself to an application of the werk principle: Thus the new organ has been designed so that all pipes of the Great are grouped centrally just below the rose window; all those of the Swell are encased behind airfoil-shaped shutters beneath the Great; those of the Choir (Ruckpositiv) are in their traditional notch in the gallery railing, while the Pedal is at either side, gathered in two symmetrical masses about the lancet windows.

Tonally this organ, like so many contemporary American instruments, has been designed with the intent of rendering the serious organ literature of all periods. The flue choruses are of Germanic inclination while the reeds are more nearly French. Both are situated and voiced to achieve in ensemble a precise attack. Despite the uneven acoustics of the building (there is unusually large absorption in the tenor register due to ceiling resonance) the sound of the full organ is warm and clear, with an overlay of complexity imparted by the reeds. For quieter effects the Choir flutes are perhaps best, enjoying as they do the benefits of "freedom of speech" and a favorable position at the gallery railing. The Swell serves well its primary use as an accompanimental division for the singers.

This is the third three-manual tracker action organ to be built in this century by an United States builder. It represents, among other things, an effort on the part of the builder to expand the formal limits of the visual in tracker organ design.

Charles Fisk in *The American Organist*, April 1966

While all segments of the organ are surrounded by reflecting panels, the instrument comes close to being "caseless" in the accepted sense, for Charles Fisk was, by his own admission, "not totally convinced of the importance of a case" in this period. But with one exception, this was the last instrument which he made with this type of visual design.

The organ in Christ Church was dedicated on June 13, 1965, with two recitals by George Faxon, separated by an Evensong Dedication Service. In the first recital Faxon was assisted by trumpeters George Kent (organist of the church) and John Pellegrino.

Opus 46, 1967
Memorial Church, Harvard University, Cambridge, Massachusetts

Great:
- Bourdon — 16′
- Prestant — 8′ (I–II)
- Spitzflute — 8′
- Octave — 4′
- Chimney Flute — 4′
- Twelfth — 2⅔′
- Fifteenth — 2′
- Cornet — II–V (mounted)
- Mixture — IV–V
- Sharp — III–IV
- Double Trumpet — 16′
- Trumpet — 8′
- Clarion — 4′

Positive:
- Violin Diapason — 8′
- Chimney Flute — 8′
- Italian Principal — 4′
- Nazard — 2⅔′
- Doublet — 2′
- Quarte de Nasard — 2′
- Tierce — 1⅗′
- Mixture — IV
- Cymbal — III
- Cremona — 8′
- English Horn — 8′

Swell:
- Spindle Flute — 8′
- Gamba — 8′
- Voix Céleste — 8′
- Gemshorn — 4′
- Night Horn — 2′
- Clarion Mixture — V
- Bassoon — 16′
- Trumpet — 8′

Choir (Rückpositiv):
- Stopped Diapason — 8′
- Prestant — 4′
- Spire Flute — 4′
- Fifteenth — 2′
- Nazard — 1⅓′
- Mixture — II–III
- Regal — 8′

Pedal:
- Prestant — 16′
- Bourdon — 16′
- Octave — 8′
- Rohrpipe — 8′
- Superoctave — 4′
- Mixture — V
- Contrabassoon — 32′ (¼ length)
- Trombone — 16′
- Trumpet — 8′
- Clarion — 4′

Couplers: Great, Positive, Swell, and Choir/Pedal; Positive, Swell, and Choir/Great; Swell/Positive

Cymbelstern, Swell Tremulant, Crescendo Pedal

Electro-pneumatic stop action with remote capture combination action (originally electro-pneumatic; changed to solid state 1983). 8 General pistons plus cancel (duplicated by toe studs), 5 pistons to each division, reversibles for Pedal couplers.

Manual compass: 61 notes; Pedal compass: 32 notes
Wind Pressure: Choir, 1⅝"; all other divisions, 2⅜"

The organ was designed in consultation with University Organist John Ferris and a distinguished committee consisting of E. Power Biggs, Edward W. Flint, Daniel Pinkham, and Donald Willing. It was first conceived as a three-manual organ to be located in the rear gallery, evolving as a four-manual when a front placement was mandated by the University administration.

Discussions between Fisk and Ferris concerning the proposed organ had begun as early as 1961, and the visual concept had begun to coalesce in Charles Fisk's mind:

> I feel more strongly than ever that the church at Harvard requires a rather elaborate case, something which brings to a focus all the somewhat senseless decoration that presently exists therein. The Baltimore case was about as elaborate as I would ever wish to be responsible for, so that we probably should think in terms of the old European way of having the case carved by a professional, if it is to be more complex than the Baltimore case.
>
> Charles Fisk to John Ferris, November 7, 1961

Fisk did in fact follow through with this idea, and the carvings, which represent sea plants and creatures (including the "sacred cod" of Bostonian lore), were executed by the Rockport artist Roger Martin.

By 1963 a preliminary drawing of the proposed organ had been submitted which depicted an organ of four manual divisions and pedal located at the front of the chancel (Appleton Chapel). An accompanying letter reveals that the tonal concept was developing along with the visual, although changes continued to be made after this—for example, early stoplists specified two enclosed divisions rather than one. A few paragraphs outline the builder's concept for each division:

> The principal tonal resources of the organ are to be found in the Great division, the pipes of which are placed in the very top of the case. Speaking as it would, directly over the rood screen and out into the nave, there

should be no question as to the capability of the Great of leading the congregation in hymn singing; this, of course, is the one truly essential requirement of the organ in respect to the Sunday services. For performance of the organ literature the Great would of course be ample.

The pipes of the Swell division are to be seen just below those of the Great. Two stops of the Swell, the 8 foot and 4 foot Principals, stand outside the expression box, whose movements, were they unscreened, would be a distraction to the congregation. The strength of the full Swell would be only a little less than that of the full Great.

Below the Swell and to either side of the keydesk are the expression shutters, or louvres, for the Echo division. Small in both size and strength, this division would be useful in accompaniment and in soft antiphonal effects.

The Choir organ, standing apart from the main case and, as it were, down among the people, would be especially appropriate for more intimate types of music. Its visual effect as a centerpiece for the chapel would be matched by its delicacy of sound, which would be that of a chamber instrument, in contrast to the massiveness of the Great, Swell, and Pedal. A particularly important use for this Choir organ would be the playing of continuo parts and the accompaniment of small groups of voices and instruments.

The Pedal division is represented by the largest pipes in the case, which belong to the 16 foot Principal. In classical fashion the Pedal is symmetrically divided, half of the pipes being in the left hand tower, the other half in the right.

Charles Fisk to John Ferris, April 22, 1963

The major change made in this early plan was the evolution of the Swell into an unenclosed division called, for want of a better name, Positive. The Echo grew proportionately, acquired some reeds, and became the Swell, but these changes occasioned little alteration of the physical layout. The basic philosophy of this organ as a consciously eclectic instrument was unchanged, and is expressed by Charles Fisk in his notes for a descriptive brochure published at the time of the dedication:

Harvard's new organ was designed with three purposes in mind: First, that the organ should provide proper accompaniment for the Sunday services in the Memorial Church; second, that it should accompany the much smaller daily services in Appleton Chapel; third, that those Harvard and Radcliffe students whose interests incline toward organ music might learn from this organ how the great wealth of literature for the instrument is intended to sound.

Experience shows that the most important feature of any organ is its placement within the room where it is to be heard. The position of this organ in front of the palladium window in Appleton Chapel was chosen with especial regard to the accompaniment of the hymns sung by the Sunday congregations, for only if an organ faces the congregation squarely will the essential rhythmic incisiveness be felt by the congregation. For the same reason, the wooden organ case is made broad and high but very shallow—it is less than four feet deep. Such a case projects the sound efficiently and prevents the organ from absorbing its own sound; moreover, it lends warmth and blend to the ensemble.

This organ is perhaps most effective in its use during the daily services within Appleton Chapel, because then the congregation, being enclosed with it in the same room, has the feeling of being surrounded by music. The congregation seated in the main church is not so fortunate since they are actually in a separate room. On the other hand, the full organ, which is scaled for the farthest reaches of the church, is likely to seem too intense to persons seated in the chapel. For these more intimate services, the organist at his discretion may use the Positive division and the mildly voiced Choir Organ.

As regards familiarizing the students with the organ literature, a conscious effort has been made to create within this single instrument the features required for the performing of all styles of serious organ music. Since such a goal has been for some years the great American dream, its realization has been often essayed. The chief difference between the present effort in eclecticism and those which have preceded it is an emphasis not on the choice of stops, but rather on the method of controlling them. The governing idea here is that any normal kind of articulate stop in an organ will be useful if it is encased and situated so as to be clearly heard, and if the player has it "at his finger tips," that is to say, if the connection between finger and pipe is direct and unencumbered. So far, the best way of assuring such connection is to employ the time honored tracker (mechanical) key action.

Charles Fisk, in *The Isham Memorial Organ,* 1968

The organ was dedicated in a morning service on December 3, 1967, and the inaugural recital was given by Anton Heiller on December 28, as part of an American Guild of Organists conclave. During the following year a series of Monday evening recitals was given by E. Power Biggs (who premiered *A Prophecy,* a commissioned work by Daniel Pinkham), Donald Willing, Vernon de Tar, Max Miller, Marian Ruhl, Herbert Burtis, Lois Pardue, and John Ferris.

One innovation attempted in this organ was the doubling of the unison ranks of the Great Principal chorus. Shortly after the completion of the organ Charles Fisk, writing to a friend, gave his rationale for this:

If it hadn't been so costly in terms of space and money I would not have minded doubling the ranks of the 8' Prestant right down to the bottom note. My real reasons for doubling were to "complicate" the sound, which otherwise becomes antiseptically simple in a dead room, and to help increase power in the treble of the foundation stops, the latter because I feel that the treble line generally should stand out above the alto, tenor and bass, just as it does in the average choir (of human voices). . . . Incidentally, with the doubled ranks in the Octave 4' and Fifteenth 2' the tuning of so large a division became so difficult that we finally cottoned off the second rank in these two registers. Only the 8' Prestant remains doubled.

Charles Fisk to Edward Flint, May 31, 1968

Other aspects of the Great chorus bothered the builder, notably the two mixtures, which actually predated the construction of the organ, having initially been installed by Fisk in the previous Aeolian-Skinner organ. In June of 1968 the Mixture IV–V and the treble of the Twelfth were replaced by new pipes of different scaling, and the second rank of the Fifteenth was removed. Fifteen years later, in the summer of 1983, the two mixtures were again reworked and combined to make a single Mixture of IV–IX ranks, and a new Nazard and Tierce were put in place of the Twelfth.

Outside of this, there has been only one other change in the organ. At the time of its building space was left for the addition of a stop in the Positive, and in 1972 a bequest from the family of a student who had recently died provided for the addition of a Quarte de Nasard 2' in this space. Charles Fisk had been experimenting with the hammering of pipe metal as described in the treatise of Dom Bedos de Celles, and wrote on the pipe order sheet, "Our first hammered stop."

The Harvard organ, because of its proximity, was, along with the organs in King's Chapel and Old West Church, one of those heard most frequently by Charles Fisk, and perhaps the one for which he had the greatest affection. It has been recorded several times, and two statements made by the builder for record jackets—one written near the end of his life—give a glimpse of his ongoing thoughts about the instrument:

> Organ builders in every century except the last have made it their ideal to build organs which combine warmest sound with purest clarity. This has been our ideal, too. While the tone of an organ must always be beautiful, clarity must be present so that the player can express what is in his mind. Warm, elegant tone is elicited from organ pipes only by keeping cutups high enough to allow the air to blow freely through the windway of each pipe. Clarity, on the other hand, derives from good placement of the organ, from proper winding according to classic principles, from the slider

chest and case. Clarity also depends on voicing that takes from the pipe its hardness, leaving only its full harmonic content and especially its chiff. Any organ that combines these elements—these eternal verities of organ building—will stand on its own merits no matter how eclectic its stoplist may be. So it is with the Harvard organ, eclectic of stoplist, broad in its ability to cover the musical literature, yet bound into a unity by subtle but eternal verities of organ building.

Charles Fisk, c. 1970, jacket notes for Heiller Plays Hindemith at Harvard, Harvard Square Records

Of the seventy or so organs we have built during my lifetime, I can safely say that none has lifted me to greater heights, or consigned me to the depths only an organ builder can know, more than this organ at Memorial Church, Harvard. An acoustically merciless building encloses the instrument, and, as if to compensate, the organ sometimes behaves like a caged animal. It can seem to fret, squabble, and throw tantrums at times; it can also soothe, cheer, and thrill beyond measure. If one asks, as many have, why this particular instrument should seem aesthetically so temperamental, my answer would be that it is by far the most sensitive, responsive, high-strung organ we have ever built. The open-flued voicing and large scales combined with shallow, open-faced casework and a very sensitive action—all of it designed to project the organ's message from the chapel where it stands into the main body of the church—puts a kind of "burden of proof" on the player that is perhaps not equaled by any other organ.

One cannot say of this organ that it is beautiful, because it becomes beautiful only in the hands of a tasteful performer with the God-given gift of touch. And touch on an organ is a real balancing act; it involves *Wind Management:* The mystery of pressing down the key and letting it go, a magic that a player who has the touch will never be able to convey to the player who does not have it.

And will our Opus 46 pass into the shadows? Yes, of course. But as long as the organ stands unchanged and is kept in good order, there will be occasions when players with the gift of touch and those within earshot will know that another small miracle has occurred.

Charles Fisk, December 1982, jacket notes for Christa Rakich's Clavieruebung Part III, Titanic Records

Opus 49, 1968
First Church of Christ, Scientist, Belmont, Massachusetts

Great:		Swell:	
Prestant	8'	Dulciana	8' (tapered)
Stopped Diapason	8'	Chimney Flute	4'
Spire Flute	4'	Principal	2'
Mixture	III	Sesquialtera	II

Pedal:
  Bourdon   16' (electric action, unified)
  (Gedeckt   8')
  (Gedeckt   4')

Couplers: Swell/Great, Swell/Pedal, Great/Pedal
Swell Tremulant, Balanced Swell Pedal
Manual compass: 56 notes; Pedal compass: 32 notes
Wind pressure: 1¾"

The Harvard organ was the first four-manual mechanical-action instrument to be made by an American builder in the twentieth century, and represented a heroic effort for a small workshop staffed by only ten people. The small Belmont organ followed closely on its heels, but was a pivotal instrument in many ways. It was the last small organ (with the exception of Frank Taylor's house organ) to have electro-pneumatic stop action or an electrically unified Pedal, and the first of its size to boast an 8' Prestant. This was, in fact, a late addition to the proposed stoplist, and in a letter of August 3, 1962 to Carl Vienot of the church, Charles Fisk stated that ". . . we feel that, both for visual and musical reasons, an eight foot Prestant is so desirable here." Elsewhere he recommended that, even though it would add to the cost, the façade pipes (Prestant) ". . . be of pure burnished tin, which is the prince of organ metals, and which would give a rather jewel-like quality to the appearance of the organ case." Like the Harvard organ, the Belmont instrument is fully encased, as indeed were nearly all subsequent Fisk organs.

The Belmont organ was dedicated on February 11, 1968, with a recital by John Ferris.

Opus 50, 1969
First Congregational Church, Winchester, Massachusetts

Great:		Swell:	
Bourdon	16'	Spire Flute	8'
Prestant	8'	Italian Principal	4'
Chimney Flute	8'	Gemshorn	4'
Octave	4'	Sesquialtera	II–III
Night Horn	4'	Furniture	IV
Twelfth	2⅔'	Cremona	8'
Fifteenth	2'		
Mixture	IV–VI (1⅓')		
Choir:		Pedal:	
Stopt Diapason	8'	Principal	16'
Quintadena	8'	Bourdon	16'
Spitzflute	4'	Gemshorn	8'
Principal	2'	Choralbass	4'
Larigot	1⅓'	Mixture	IV
Cymbal	II	Bassoon	16'

Couplers: Swell/Great, Choir/Great, Swell/Choir, Great/Pedal, Swell/Pedal, Choir/Pedal

Swell Tremulant, Balanced Swell Pedal, Crescendo Pedal

Harp, Chimes (from former organ)

Combinations (electric): 4 to Great, 3 to Swell, Choir, and Pedal, 4 General (duplicated by toe studs), Great to Pedal Reversible, Cancel

Manual compass: 61 notes; Pedal compass: 32 notes

Wind Pressure: 2⅜"

Over objections of Charles Fisk and the church's organist, the church insisted that the organ be placed on one side of a rather wide chancel, rather than in the rear gallery. Determined to recess as little of the organ into the chamber as possible, Fisk designed a very shallow and wide instrument, partially projecting out from the wall, and essentially unencased. The Swell stands directly behind the very shallow Choir, while the Great is above, fitted with a slanted reflecting panel to project the sound out, and the Pedal is divided at the sides. Although, due to favorable acoustics, the organ proved more successful than had been anticipated, the difficulties encountered in achieving that success confirmed Charles Fisk's conviction never to build an organ in such a location again.

The stoplist of the organ was drawn up in collaboration with Bruce Bennett, organist of the church, but owes much to the concept of the two previous three-manual organs (Opera 44 and 45). A few sets of pipes from the previous organ (a much-rebuilt Hook instrument) were revoiced and re-used, including the Pedal and Great Bourdons, the Choir Stopt Diapason, and the Great Trumpet. In a departure from usual practice, spotted metal was used for the Great Prestant. Of this organ, Charles Fisk wrote:

> This organ has from the start been viewed by its designers as a working instrument whose primary duty, aside from voluntaries, would be the accompaniment of hymns and choir anthems. Despite its expansive appearance and abundant sound, it is not a large instrument, having but twenty-seven registers, and this, together with its orthogonal placement, originally led to subdued expectations as to its potentialities for recital use. During final voicings it became clear that the organ is more versatile and projects more clearly than expected, and hence may well acquire status as a recital instrument.
>
> Charles Fisk in dedication brochure, June 1969

The organ was dedicated in a festive musical service on the morning of May 11, 1969 which included Maurice Duruflé's *Requiem* and *O Clap Your Hands* by Ralph Vaughan Williams. This was followed by an evening recital by Bruce Bennett. True to Charles Fisk's prediction, the organ has since been employed many times in recitals.

Opus 51, 1968
Zion Mennonite Church, Souderton, Pennsylvania

Great:		Choir:	
Principal	8'	Bourdon	8'
Gemshorn	8'	Chimney Flute	4'
Octave	4'	Principal	2'
Night Horn	4'	Sesquialtera	II
Mixture	IV–V	Cymbel	II
Cremona	8'		

Pedal:	
Subbass	16'
Flute	8'
Choralbass	4'
Bassoon	16'

Couplers: Great/Pedal, Choir/Pedal, Choir/Great
Tremulant
Manual compass: 56 notes; Pedal compass: 32 notes
Wind pressure: 1¾"

At the time this organ was contracted for, the church's building was still in the design stage, and here, for the first time, Charles Fisk was able to work in collaboration with an architect—Edward A. Sövik—who was interested in the organ as a visual object and open to new ideas. The spare but graceful design of the case and the favorable acoustical climate of the building were thus achieved by organ builder and architect in an atmosphere of mutual respect. In a letter to Sövik written in the early stages of planning, Fisk outlined some of his thoughts on space and acoustics:

> It is almost axiomatic with me that a church building should be as high-ceilinged as practicable. In this particular instance I would worry (usually) that a room would seem too "garage-like" if the ceiling is low, while acoustically a low ceiling tends to ground (reflect) the initial sound waves into the audience too soon for the reverberation of the room to have a chance to "play with" the sound. Height in a building permits multiple sound reflections amongst hard surfaces before absorption in the audience can take place.
>
> Usually a high ceiling is required to give adequate reverberation in a room. Because you have a large area of floor which is not to be covered by seating, it appears that adequate reverberation can be achieved without great height, but reverberation is by no means the whole story in room acoustics. If the reverberant field has inadequate excitation from the musical sources it cannot have its proper effect on the music.
>
> As far as appearance of the organ is concerned, I think a higher ceiling is preferable, although the plain truth is that the instrument planned can be designed to fit under a relatively low ceiling, simply because it will have no pipes longer than ten feet.
>
> Charles Fisk to Edward A. Sövik, March 5, 1965

Two years later, when design work on both building and organ was well under way, Fisk sent a drawing of the organ and photographs of the design model to Sövik, with a description of the organ layout and questions about the finish of the oak case.

> Our general idea in designing this organ was to produce something simple which would go well with the column it stands behind. Since the cross is centered in the room, we thought it would be best to have the organ face the cross, as if to direct the attention directed to the organ back to the center of the room.
>
> Charles Fisk to Edward A. Sövik, September 28, 1967

A year later the organ was completed and Fisk could state to a member of Sövik's firm: "We ourselves feel that it is one of our most successful instruments."

> A good part of the reason for the organ's tonal success is the building's acoustics, which for music are simply elegant when the building is empty, and of course the location of the organ within the room is also ideal. Your firm is to be congratulated for a splendid job. I was especially impressed with the visual qualities of the building which seem to live up to a current ideal in a way that few new church buildings can manage, and I was grateful to see that the organ, which might inadvertently have become a visual focal point, seemed not to obtrude upon the serenity of the place.
> Charles Fisk to Kenneth Peterson, October 4, 1968

Opus 52, 1968
St. Paul's Roman Catholic Church, Greencastle, Indiana

Manual:		Pedal:	
Spitzprincipal	8'	Bourdon	16'
Chimney Flute	4'		
Fifteenth	2'		

Coupler: Manual/Pedal
Manual compass: 56 notes; Pedal compass: 32 notes

This organ was designed to be an adjunct to the two-manual "Wellesley" style organ placed in the church's gallery in 1965, and was located in the chancel of the church. In his proposal Charles Fisk points out the difference between the two:

> In specification this organ is a little unusual in that it uses an open (tapered) manual foundation stop instead of a stopped flute; this in order to give fulness for hymn accompaniment. The sound of the organ would also be enough different from that of the gallery organ to be refreshing.
> Charles Fisk to Rev. Francis Kull, October 22, 1964

Much of the design and construction work on this organ was entrusted to Herman Greunke, an employee of several years' experience. It was later moved to St. Meinrad's Seminary, St. Meinrad, Indiana.

Opus 54, 1971
First Church of Christ (Center Church), New Haven, Connecticut

Great:		Choir (Rückpositiv):	
Bourdon	16' (wood)	Chimney Flute	8'
Prestant	8' (I–II)	Dulciana	8'
Stopped Flute	8' (wood)	Prestant	4'
Octave	4'	Spindle Flute	4'
Twelfth	2⅔'	Doublet	2'
Fifteenth	2'	Sesquialtera	II
Blockflute	2'	Sharp	IV
Septierce	II–III	Cremona	8'
Mixture	IV–VI		
Trumpet	8'		
Clarion	4'		

Echo (enclosed; added 1974):		Pedal:	
Spire Flute	8'	Subbass	16'
Flute Céleste	8'	Octave	8'
Chimney Flute	4'	Rohrpipe	8'
Principal	2'	Superoctaves	II
Cornet	II–III	Mixture	IV
Cymbal	II	Bassoon	16'
Hautboy	8'	Trumpet	8'

Couplers: Great/Pedal, Choir/Pedal, Echo/Pedal, Choir/Great, Echo/Great, Echo/Choir

General Tremulant, Swell pedal (Echo), Crescendo pedal

Combinations: 4 General, 10 Divisional, Cancel, Great to Pedal Reversible

Manual compass: 61 notes; Pedal compass: 32 notes

Center Church, never designed to house an organ, has a very shallow gallery. Previous instruments had been deeply recessed into a steeple chamber, something Fisk was determined not to do:

> ... the builders felt it imperative that the sound-producing portions of the instrument be located within the four walls of the auditorium. The result has been a design in which the Great, Echo, and Pedal are located in a broad but shallow case against a newly made back wall in the gallery, with the Choir division in Ruckpositiv position on the gallery rail. The only portions of the organ now in the steeple area are the blower and bellows.
>
> Charles Fisk, in *The Diapason*, December 1972

The organ case is based on classic North German lines, and contains the first embossed front pipes to be employed in a Fisk organ. Economy dictated the re-use of a few rebuilt ranks of pipes from the church's former Austin organ (notably the open wood Subbass which forms the façade of the Pedal towers) and the deferment of the completion of the Echo division. Originally conceived as a Brustwerk similar to that of the King's Chapel organ, it evolved into a small Swell division.

> The object of the change in specification is to be sure that the Brustwerk [Echo] does not have stops which duplicate the function of those elsewhere in the organ. For example, in the Great you have already a Stopped Flute which has turned out very much like the Stopped Diapason we had planned for the Brustwerk, whereas you have no 8 foot tapered flute. It is a good sound to have, and works well for the basis of a Brustwerk. A 4' Rohrflute goes very well with an 8' Spire Flute. The Larigot 1⅓' would give you a mutation possibility which you presently lack. A light Mixture would be in contrast to the two rather strong Mixtures presently in the Great and Choir. Instead of a Regal 16', which would be nice, I have specified an 8' Hautboy (a somewhat nasal Oboe stop). The Choir Cremona 8' is wiry enough to serve the occasional need for a Regal, and you need an enclosed solo voice. This Hautboy would be made according to the directions given by Dom Bedos.
>
> Charles Fisk to Jack Litten, June 6, 1972

The Center Church organ, dedicated to former organist Pauline Voorhees, was opened on November 7, 1971, with a morning service followed by an afternoon recital played by Charles Krigbaum.

Opus 55, 1971
Old West Church (United Methodist), Boston, Massachusetts

Great:		
Bourdon	(wood)	16'
Prestant		8'
Spire Flute		8'
Octave		4'
Doublet		2'
Sesquialter		II
Mixture		IV–VI
Trumpet		8'
Clarion		4'

Swell:		
Violin Diapason		8'
Stopt Diapason	(wood)	8'
Spitz Flute		4'
Cornet		III
Fourniture		III
Contra Hautboy		16'
Trumpet		8'

Choir (Rückpositiv):	
Chimney Flute	8'
Prestant	4'
Night Horn	4'
Nazard	II
Fifteenth	2'
Sharp	IV
Cremona	8'

Pedal:		
Subbass	(stopped wood)	16'
Octave		8'
Rohrpipe		8'
Superoctaves		4' & 2'
Mixture		III
Trombone		16'

Couplers: Swell/Great, Choir/Great, Swell/Choir, Great/Pedal, Swell/Pedal, Choir/Pedal
General Tremulant, Balanced Swell Pedal, Crescendo Pedal
Combinations: 4 General, 2 Divisional to each manual, Tutti Great, Cancel Great, General Cancel, Great to Pedal Reversible
Manual compass: 61 notes; Pedal compass: 32 notes
Wind pressure: 2¼"

This instrument is one of the smallest three-manual organs ever made by Fisk, yet it has proven over the years to be surprisingly flexible for the proper interpretation of a wide range of musical styles. Economy dictated the small size and the re-use of a few sets of rebuilt pipes from a previous small Cole instrument, largely in the Swell and Pedal. The second rank of the Nazard (a Tierce) was something of an afterthought; of incomplete compass, it can be added or subtracted manually even though the stop action is electrical. The main case is a reworking of a mahogany case built c. 1830 and attributed to Thomas Appleton, which was found in a church in Ipswich that was being torn down. The central section has been replaced by two towers; the Choir case is entirely new. The Great Trumpet 8′ was the first set of reed pipes to be made in the Fisk workshop.

> The Old West Church was designed by the well-known architect Asher Benjamin and built in 1806. Though somewhat altered, it still possesses the grace and beauty of an urbane Federal meeting house. In designing an organ for this church . . . we felt strongly that there should be three manuals, even though funds were limited, and we felt that the case should if possible possess the same gracious qualities as the building. Good fortune brought us fragments of a case by the organ builder Thomas Appleton . . . . Taking Appleton's case as a kernel we evolved a case design from which, we hope, both men might have drawn satisfaction had they lived to see it. Housed within the case is an organ of twenty-nine stops which makes a valiant effort to cover the full gamut of the organ literature, and may even succeed in doing so. It is aided in this by the acoustics of the West Church, which though by no means ideal, are free enough to permit the mind to imagine how ideal acoustics might sound.
>
> Charles Fisk, notes for a recording of Buxtehude works by Mireille Lagacé, 1975

As in virtually all of Fisk's organs up to this point, there is a strong French classic bias to the basic tonal design, eclectic though this may be in overall concept. In another set of jacket notes, Charles Fisk delineated his underlying rationale for this:

> When Melville Smith was alive, one's chief joy in building an organ lay in the knowledge that someday one might hear him play upon it. Whenever I personally was in process of designing or voicing, the sound of his playing—his inimitable touching of the keys—was constantly in my head. Each organ was thus in some measure made for him, for his art, under his influence. Indeed, a number of our organs came into being through his direct influence: King's Chapel, the large organ at Harvard, the small organ at Wellesley College and the organ in [the Unitarian Church in] Newburyport; each is in part the result of his efforts. The organ heard on this recording, that of the Old West Church, Boston, was never known to him, yet it is perhaps the organ he would have enjoyed most. Certainly we have tried to make it so. Many heterogeneous elements went into its construction—parts of an 1835 case by Thomas Appleton (though the case is mostly new), a basic facade design from the 17th century English builder Bernhard Smith, new carvings by James McClellan, certain stops from various old organs, along with a great deal else that is new—and yet the conception is essentially Alsatian and is most closely related to the single Andreas Silbermann organ that Melville Smith loved above all others: Marmoutier. The chorus scalings are Marmoutier; so are

the voicing and the unskived upper lips, the tin bodies and lead feet of the *principalia*, the Parisian style reeds—all are, as it were, appointed to please our deceased friend. How fitting it is that this recording, which sets forth the sounds of an organ made as though for Melville Smith, should be played by his most favored disciple, Frank Taylor, a person of rare musical gift, one in whom Melville Smith's art still lives. And how appropriate that the music too should be Smith's favorite, the stuff that he first brought us to learn, and eventually to know, and finally to love as though it were our own.

Charles Fisk, notes for a recording of DuMage and D'Andrieu works
by Frank Taylor, c. 1974

The organ was dedicated on Easter Day, 1971, with a recital by Dr. Max Miller.

Opus 56, 1971
Trinity Episcopal Church, Collinsville, Connecticut

Manual:		Pedal:	
Prestant	8′	Bourdon	16′
Stopped Diapason	8′ (divided)	(Bassoon	16′)
Spire Flute	4′ (divided)	(Hautboy	8′)
Fifteenth	2′		
Sesquialtera	II (divided)		
Mixture	IV		
Hautboy	16′ (treble)		
Bassoon	16′ (bass)		

Coupler: Manual/Pedal
Tremulant (hand lever)
Machine stop to Fifteenth & Mixture
Manual compass: 61 notes; Pedal compass: 32 notes
The divided stops divide at middle C; the reed stop is mechanically borrowed by the Pedal.

This organ was designed in response to a need for a small instrument that was simple, yet flexible and elegant. It was the first Fisk organ in which a manual stop was made available in the Pedal by non-electric "transmission," and the smallest to boast a full-compass 8′ Prestant.

The pipework is enclosed in a shallow mahogany case which serves to focus the sound of the instrument and to enhance the cohesiveness of its several voices. The shape of the graceful case with its hand-carved pipe shades is derived from and directly related to the arrangement of the pipes on the windchest. The tonal design of the organ has been made according to classic principles which give it a rich full *pleno* (or full organ) on the one hand while allowing a diversity of timbres and tonal combinations on the other.

Charles Fisk, notes supplied for dedication program, 1971

The organ was dedicated in a service and recital the afternoon of October 24, 1971. The recital of baroque, romantic and modern German music was given by Dr. George Becker, organist, and Grieg Shearer, flautist.

Opus 57, 1972
St. Paul's Episcopal Church, Willimantic, Connecticut

Great:		Swell:	
Bourdon	16'	Diapason	8' (prepared for)
Prestant	8'	Stopt Diapason	8'
Chimney Flute	8'	Flute	4' (open wood)
Italian Principal	4'	Doublet	2'
Fifteenth	2' (prepared for)	Sharp	IV
{ Nazard	2⅔'	Tertian	II (prepared for)
{ Cornet	II–III	Cremona	8'
Mixture	VI–VIII		
Trumpet	8'		

Pedal:	
Bourdon	16' (from Great)
Octave	8' (from Great)
Sackbut	16'
Trumpet	8' (from Great)

Couplers: Great/Pedal, Choir/Pedal, Choir/Great
Tremulant, Cymbalstar
Machine stop affecting Great Mixture and Trumpet
Manual compass: 61 notes; Pedal compass: 32 notes

The bracketed pair of stops in the Great ({) is a double-drawing stop; drawing the stopknob halfway produces the 2⅔′ rank alone and drawing it full adds the other ranks which make up the Cornet. This was Fisk's first use of this device, which appears in many later organs. In this organ he again made use of mechanical "transmissions" in the Pedal, the only independent Pedal rank being the 16′ reed. The three "prepared–for" stops were installed in 1977.

The Choir division was actually a Brustwerk provided with swell shutters. The case design and basic layout were subsequently used, in modified form, in two other organs.

> The case of the "Alleluia Organ"—as Mrs. Hale requested it be named—is a single unit; a high, wide, shallow cabinet of catspaw-figured natural oak with burnished tin pipes in the facade and the mahogany keydesk built into the lower face. The naturals are made of grenadil, the sharps of rosewood topped with ivory and the faces of the stop knobs are hand-engraved ivory.
>
> In this organ Charles Fisk has employed a tonal design rather different than the usual "Bach-style" approach of our time. The design for this instrument is more like that of organs which were already old in Bach's day and which the Master knew very well. Such organs were conceived as instruments of two divisions only, the Great and Pedal forming one division and the Choir, or Positive, forming the other. In all early instruments it was customary to play the bass part on the manuals instead of on the pedals. With this organ it is possible to do either and this opens up new possibilities for the performance of early music, especially the music of France before and during Bach's time. To further secure the possibilities for the French classic literature, the Trumpet and Cremona stops in this organ are direct copies of the work of François-Henry Cliquot, the last of the French classic builders, who patiently completed his last and greatest effort in the Cathedral of Poitiers while the French Revolution raged around him.
>
> Charles Fisk, notes supplied for dedication program, 1972

The Alleluia Organ was dedicated in a choral evensong service on the afternoon of September 24, 1972, in which the music was provided by Mrs. Kenneth Moorhead, the church's organist. This was followed by a series of recitals given on the first Sundays of the three subsequent months by George Becker, Cameron Johnson, and Virginia Herrmann.

Opus 62, 1974
Ascension Memorial Church, Ipswich, Massachusetts

Great:		Swell:		
Bourdon	16'	Diapason		8'
Prestant	8' (I–II)	Stopped Diapason		8'
Chimney Flute	8'	Flute	(chimney)	4'
Octave	4'	Octave		2'
Doublet	2'	Larigot		1⅓'
Night Horn	2'	Sharp		IV
Sesquialtera	II	Cromorne		8'
Mixture	IV–V			
Trumpet	8'			
Clarion	4'			

Pedal:	
Principal	16'
Flute	8'
Superoctave	4'
Bassoon	16'
Trumpet	8'

Couplers: Great/Pedal, Swell/Pedal, Swell/Great
Tremulant, Balanced Swell Pedal
Manual compass: 61 notes; Pedal compass: 32 notes

In design, this organ was an expanded version of the Willimantic organ, with the "Brustwerk" enlarged to a full-fledged Swell division, an independent Pedal located behind the main case, and a detached console. Of it Fisk wrote:

> The new organ is a two-manual instrument of such moderate size as befits a parish church. Like all church organs, its main purpose is to lead the hymns, to accompany the choir anthems and to help the congregation in its liturgical responses. In addition, it is designed to play much of the great organ literature, and especially the literature of the 17th and 18th centuries. In certain ways the new organ specializes: For example, the manual trumpets are made of tin according to the drawings of the 18th century French organ builder François-Henri Clicquot, and are the first in this country to employ the old practice of hammering the metal sheets before rolling them up into resonators. The clang of these trumpets is bold and pungent. At the same time, the particular case design here enhances the blend of these trumpets with the flue work, so that the sound of full organ

is a tightly woven fabric. Mechanical (tracker) key and stop actions insure that this sound can be deftly controlled by the organist, and a detached keydesk has been provided so that the organist can be in complete command of the choir, whose members surround the keydesk. Quite unusual are the Swell shutters placed within the Brustwerk-style doors, allowing either expression by pedal or complete opening of the doors for maximum sound.

Charles Fisk, in descriptive flyer, 1974

The organ was dedicated on December 2, 1974, with a recital by French organist André Isoir.

Opus 64, 1974
University of Minnesota, Minneapolis, Minnesota

Manual:
    Stopt Diapason   8'
    Chimney Flute   4'
    Principal   2'
    Regal   8'

Machine stop for Principal and Regal
Compass: 56 notes
All stops divide at middle C

This was the first positive organ to be built by the Fisk firm since Daniel Pinkham's three-stop instrument, completed in 1961. It was the result of considerable rethinking on the subject of positives by Charles Fisk, and combines both English and German tonal concepts.

> A departure from the usual layout of such instruments is the location of the keyboard at one end. For ensemble playing, this has the advantage of allowing the player improved visibility as well as the opportunity to hear the tonal balance more accurately. The location of the stopknobs above the keyboard allows the case to be only slightly wider than the keyboard.... The case is actually wedge-shaped, in the manner of a harpsichord. The upper part of the instrument may be removed from the lower part for moving.
>
> Charles Fisk, publicity release, 1974

Opus 65, 1974
Church of the Epiphany, Winchester, Massachusetts

Great:
    Prestant   8′
    Gemshorn   8′
    Octave   4′
    Chimney Flute   4′
    { Fifteenth   2′ (prepared for)
    { Cornet   III (prepared for)
    Mixture   IV–VI
    Trumpet   8′ (prepared for)

Choir (enclosed):
    Open Diapason   8′ (prepared for)
    Stopt Diapason   8′
    Spitzflute   4′
    Octave   2′
    { Nazard   2 2/3′
    { Sesquialter   II
    Cymbal   II (prepared for)
    Cremona   8′ (placed in Great temporarily)

Pedal:
    Subbass   16′
    Gemshorn   8′ (from Great, prepared for)
    Bassoon   16′

Couplers: Great/Pedal, Choir/Pedal, Choir/Great
Tremulant, Balanced Swell Pedal
Manual compass: 56 notes; Pedal compass: 30 notes
Bracketed stops are double-drawing

    This was the third organ to be built with the basic case design of the Willimantic organ. Like that instrument, it contains the Pedal stops within the upper case; like the Ipswich instrument it has an enlarged Brustwerk/Swell (called Choir) and a detached console.

    The instrument we would be building for you would be rather different from the instrument we have built for the Congregational Church in your city. The latter was designed as a small but comprehensive three-manual organ admittedly compromised by its location in the building. Yours, though even smaller, would be greatly enhanced by its balcony location, and would have about it a purity and economy of effect which could set a new standard for Episcopal churches in our area. In my opinion, such a standard needs to be set. Churchmen everywhere need to be shown that, in organs, a clear statement that combines brevity and excellence is the answer for today.

Charles Fisk to Richard N. Carr, October 26, 1970

The organ was dedicated in a Festival Service held April 28, 1974, during which Bach's Cantata 29 *(Wir danken dir, Gott)* was performed by the choir under the direction of Carl S. Fudge. The "prepared-for" Great and Pedal stops were added in 1983.

NEW ENGLAND CONSERVATORY, BOSTON, MASSACHUSETTS: Opus 66, 1974

Opus 66A, 1974
Yale School of Music, New Haven, Connecticut

Manual:
Stopped Diapason	8' (wood, divided)
Principal	4' (open wood)
Fifteenth	2' (divided)
Twenty-second	1'
Cornet Treble	II
Mixture Treble	II
Sesquialtera Bass	II

Machine stop to bring on or retire upperwork
Compass: 55 notes, GG, AA, CC-e^3

These two "twin" instruments have a case design virtually identical to that of the four-stop positive built for the University of Minnesota, but a significantly different stoplist and orientation.

> The Conservatory's new chamber organ, while conceived as an all-purpose chamber instrument, with continuo playing as a specialty, draws its inspiration from the work of John Snetzler, the eighteenth century Swiss who spent most of his professional life in England. Snetzler built a great many chamber organs and in so doing brought the English chamber organ to a pinnacle of refinement, especially as regards delicacy of tone. The Conservatory's instrument employs extensively the pipe scales and

forms found in the 1761 Snetzler presently in the possession of the Smithsonian Institution. The voicing techniques also follow Snetzler's example, as does the flexible winding of the instrument. Like the Smithsonian Snetzler, the organ has its stops divide just below middle C, making possible a difference of sonority between the left and right hands, much as if the organ possessed two manuals. Snetzler's machine stop pedal is also included; when depressed this device disconnects the upperwork, making echo effects possible, again almost as though the instrument had two manuals instead of one.

While Snetzler's work serves as the tonal model, the physical shape of the Conservatory's instrument is new and represents adaptation to modern needs. The keyboard is placed on one end (instead of on the side as is customary) in order that the organist may hear correct balance in ensemble and be able to see the conductor without using a mirror. Also, the player need not place his back to an audience. Cupboard doors have been fitted to both sides of the cabinet so that the organ, unlike the piano or harpsichord, may be situated at either stage right or stage left and still project its sound toward the audience.

Charles Fisk, "Statement by the Organ Builder," 1974

The New England Conservatory organ was opened in a program of solo and concerted music in Jordan Hall on March 4, 1974; the Yale instrument has been used in similar concerts.

Opus 67, 1976
Central Christian Church, Huntington, Indiana

Great:		Swell:	
Bourdon	16'	Geigen (prepared for)	8'
Prestant	8'	Chimney Flute	8'
Spire Flute	8'	Spitz Flute	4'
Octave	4'	⎰ Nazard	2⅔'
Doublet (prepared for)	2'	⎱ Sesquialtera	II
⎰ Blockflute	2'	⎰ Fifteenth	2'
⎱ Cornet	III	⎱ Fourniture	IV
Mixture	IV–VI	Cremona	8'
Trumpet	8'	Hautbois (prepared for)	8'

Pedal:
    Bourdon   16'
    Octave   8'
    ⎰ Superoctave   4'
    ⎱ Superoctaves   II
    Bassoon   16'

Couplers: Swell/Great, Great/Pedal, Swell/Pedal
Tremulant (Tremblant Doux)
Balanced Swell Pedal
Manual compass: 56 notes; Pedal compass: 30 notes
Wind Pressure: 2¼"
Bracketed stops are double-drawing

    Located in a contemporary building, the physical style of this organ was a departure from much of the preceding work. The tonal concept, however, still derives from Charles Fisk's Alsatian ideal, now tinged with a growing interest in the work of Gottfried Silbermann. As with previous organs, eclecticism is an important element.

> Central Christian Church's new organ is a completely unique musical instrument, designed to do many things. Its first purpose is to encourage the congregation to sing the hymns. Secondly, it must accompany the singing of the choir and provide quiet musical interludes for the liturgy of this church. And, finally, it must play organ music, that is, music written expressly for the organ—the organ literature. For an instrument of this size, this is no small task; indeed, organ builders face no greater challenge

than that of compacting much versatility into an instrument of modest proportions.

This organ is unique in ways other than musical ones. Its singular visual design is carefully keyed to the architecture of the church. In fact, the organ case seems physically "keyed" into a V-shaped notch in the ceiling provided by the architect, and the entire design flows from elements already present in the architecture. At the top of the case is the Swell division, connected to the upper keyboard and enclosed by vertical shutters, which are moved by the organist's foot. The scaffold below the Swell is for access to the Swell pipework; for the eye, its narrow planks echo the staves placed against the wall behind the pulpit. Midway below are the silvery pipes of the Great Prestant, standing in a random arrangement of shadow boxes, and below the rest are the sombre wooden pipes of the Pedal Bourdon. These latter give the organ its deepest tones; it is thus fitting that they occur, like a foundation, near the floor.

In building this organ, we have endeavored to provide for the direct musical needs of this church. At the same time, we have tried to make possible music from epochs other than our own. The world of church music spans centuries; this organ, despite its contemporary appearance, reaches far back into the musical past for its inspiration. Perhaps our most enduring purpose is to show how full of life the best church music has always been.

Charles Fisk, in dedication booklet, 1976

The organ was dedicated on October 3, 1976, with morning services and an afternoon recital by Joan Lippincott. The recitalist had requested a tonal description of the organ, and Charles Fisk responded with the following:

GREAT

Bourdon 16': A bit assertive and full, a good stop for the Plein Jeu.

Prestant 8': Rather big, foundational yet developed, too loud for accompaniments, a good solo stop by itself.

Spire Flute 8': Melts in your mouth, *very* limp and quite gushy with the tremulant (in a quiet way), a very good accompaniment to Swell solos.

Octave 4': The usual partner to the Prestant, quite full, not sharp.

Blockflute 2': (on a half-draw from the Cornet) Too wide to go with the chorus, not especially loud, goes well with 8' Spire Flute, possible use in louder trios.

Cornet II: $2\frac{2}{3}'-2'-1\frac{3}{5}'$ from tenor D$\sharp$ upward (below that it is $2'-1\frac{3}{5}'-1\frac{1}{3}'$ to save space on chest). Moderately broad in scale, a good Great Cornet; bass is strong enough to be used in a tierce en taille, even below the break.

Mixture IV–VI: Our usual strong $1\frac{1}{3}'$ mixture, somewhat full and not too scratchy.

Trumpet 8': A small scale version of what's in the West Church, quite nice, free. French shallots. Makes the Great chorus very rigid but doesn't quite overpower it. It adds both mass and frazz in abundance.

SWELL, located above Great next to ceiling; shutters are obvious to onlookers, and open very wide.

Chimney Flute 8': Big metal stop, limp but of definite character. A contrast to the Great 8' flute in timbre.

Spitzflute 4': An AC/DC stop reminiscent of G. D. Harrison, more of a principal than a flute. It doesn't attract all by itself but makes a good quarterback for the division. You'll use it all the time.

Nazard 2⅔': (half-draw from Sesquialtera) Very flutey, O.K. for trios, but we strengthened the bass to make it suitable for jeux de tierces.

Octave 2': (half-draw from Fourniture) Our usual starchy secondary manual two foot stop. Same as Positive 2' at Harvard.

Sesquialtera II: Throughgoing flutey 2⅔' and 1⅗', about like the Harvard Positive mutations.

Fourniture IV: Quite tingly and, because of position, a real addition to the Great chorus when coupled.

Cremona 8': Our usual French style, not a shrinking violet because it's right in front of the Swell. Turned out very well and should be useful both in chorus and as a solo.

PEDAL, located in the bottom of the instrument.

Bourdon 16': Our usual wood stop, quinty but solid, works well for everything and can, once in a while, be used alone if the manual texture is right.

Octave 8': Metal, like the European models, O.K. for trios, not edgy at all, quite full.

Octave 4': (half-draw from Superoctaves 4' and 2'). Like the 8'.

Octaves 4' & 2': The 2' rank adds emphasis to the 4' and gives some semblance of an independent pedal.

Bassoon 16': Essentially a honky Clarinet or Cromorne of large scale, uneven sounding by itself but very quick, a good strong underpinning for the Pedal.

Tremblant Doux: Affects everything and changes its beat depending on how it is used. It quits if you have too many stops, is very sexy if you choose just the right stops.

The wind system is quite "advanced," i.e., it is in Gottfried Silbermann's measurements and therefore does not respond happily to big 19th century French pieces with ten-note chords. If you want, I can shorten the duct from bellows to organ in ten minutes so the big pieces will sound O.K. but then the earlier stuff suffers and the tremolo loses its charm . . . ."

Charles Fisk to Joan Lippincott, August 5, 1976

The three "prepared-for" stops were installed in February of 1986, and first used on Easter Sunday of that year. They are dedicated to the memory of Patricia Ann Enos, who had chaired the original organ committee.

Opus 68, 1976
University of Vermont Recital Hall, Burlington, Vermont

Great:		Positive:	
Double Open Diapason	16'	Bourdon	8'
Double Stopped Diapason	16'	Prestant	4'
Principal	8'	Doublet	2'
Bourdon	8'	Quarte de Nasard	2'
Octave	4'	Larigot	1⅓'
Chimney Flute	4'	Sesquialtera	I & II
Double Tierce	3⅕'	Fourniture	IV
Doublet	2'	Cromorne	8'
Cornet	I & III	Récit:	
Grosse Fourniture	VI & VIII	Cornet	V
Trumpet	8'		
Voix Humaine	8'		
Clarion	4'		

Pedal:	
Prestant	16'
Flute	8'
Flute	4'
Night Horn	2'
Bassoon	16'
Trumpet	8'

Couplers: Great/Pedal, Positive/Pedal, Positive/Great
General Tremulant (Tremblant Doux)
Manual compass: 56 notes; Pedal compass: 30 notes
Wind Pressure: 2⁵⁄₁₆"
Great Cornet and Fourniture and Positive Sesquialtera are double-drawing

This organ was initially conceived as a rather "standard" Fisk organ, but encouragement from consultant Fenner Douglass, and perhaps also the successful experience of basing Opus 66 on a definite historical model, led to a decision to redesign it along strong French classic lines:

I must confess I was not happy with the stop list that we originally appended to the contract. The Pedal seemed much larger than necessary (for a long time I have felt that modern American pedal organs were too large) and I sensed that there were redundancies in the manuals, at least as I conceived the stops listed.

I also have had the abiding feeling that the UVM organ must draw a certain special integrity from somewhere. This is not easy in the case of a small instrument, especially if one attempts to make it perform every scrap of organ literature. In a teaching, non-church instrument I think the thread of integrity is absolutely essential if the student is to be given the conception we wish above all for him to receive.

Fenner's fine Italian hand is clearly present in the design as it now stands, and I am sure no one of us is more interested than he is in the notion that an organ design should spring from a single classical model, and should certainly not attempt to become just another version of the "American Classic Organ." I must say that my good sense tells me he is absolutely right in this, and in truth, although our organs in the past have appeared eclectic, they have all sprung from the *Klang ideal* of the Alsatian builder Andreas Silbermann, whose work I have never been able to get out of my head. If our organs have shown unusual ability to bring to life both French and German music, I suppose it is because the chosen model itself stands on the border between the two countries. Frankly, I do not ever expect to escape the Alsatian ideal, and perhaps that is good, because the sound is beautiful beyond recall.

Charles Fisk to James Chapman, September 11, 1973

This organ was the first Fisk instrument to employ a full-length 16' Principal on a manual division, and the second to be tuned in Kirnberger III temperament (the first being the organ in Ipswich). In physical design, it employed the device of a "suspended" Positive division, cantilevered forward of the main case, but above the keydesk. This arrangement was first used in the Souderton instrument, and would later be used for the large organ in Rochester, New York. The casework is of classical layout, but with simple contemporary pipe shades and trim, to harmonize with the room. Although the disposition of this organ is more directly inspired by the French baroque aesthetic than any previous Fisk instrument, it is not a direct copy, and its builder was as aware as ever of the need for a certain eclecticism:

> And all the while this instrument is being designed to play the full gamut of organ literature through the year 1825. The only music that will not be playable is that small portion of the 19th century repertoire that cannot be played without a swell box.
>
> Charles Fisk to William C. Metcalfe, June 25, 1975

During the period in which this organ and some of those immediately preceding it were built, Charles Fisk had been putting into practice his theories concerning flexible wind supply derived from his studies of historic instruments. Wedge-shaped bellows and internal tremulants (the French *Tremblant Doux*) had become fairly standard, and of the tremulant in the University of Vermont organ he wrote:

> That Tremulant is simply a copy of what I found in Gottfried Silbermann's organs in East Germany. He used a big oak pallet like that, but of course his oak isn't as heavy as ours, so I ended up boring holes in ours to make it lighter. Silbermann's tremulants were by far the most beautiful I can remember hearing, so luscious I could hardly bear to turn them off. UVM's tremulant isn't that good, but it has its points. I'm sure the sizes of the wind ducts and the pallet boxes are more important than the details of the tremulant. Really, the whole wind system *is* the tremulant.
>
> Charles Fisk to Hellmuth Wolff, March 12, 1976

The University of Vermont organ was inaugurated on February 22, 1976, with a program of French and German music played by Fenner Douglass.

Opus 69, 1975
St. Michael's Episcopal Church, Marblehead, Massachusetts

Great:
- Bourdon 16'
- Open Diapason 8'
- Stopped Diapason 8'
- Principal 4'
- Flute (open wood) 4'
- Fifteenth 2'
- Cornet III
- Mixture IV–V
- Trumpet 8'

Swell:
- Spire Flute 8'
- Flute Céleste (tenor C) 8'
- Chimney Flute 4'
- Flageolet 2'
- Sesquialtera II
- Sharp IV
- Hautboy 8'

Pedal:
- Sub Bass (stopped wood) 16'
- Flûte 8'
- Octave 4'
- Mixture III
- Bassoon 16'

Couplers: Swell/Great, Swell/Pedal, Great/Pedal
Tremulant, Cymbal Star
Manual compass: 61 notes; Pedal compass: 32 notes

The design of this organ was a return to a more "all-purpose" concept, partially dictated by the use of the organ in a very active liturgical music program. It was the first organ to employ electric stop and combination action since 1971 (Opus 55). Housed in a small but pleasing "gothick" case of 1833 by E. & G. G. Hook, it is so arranged that the Swell occupies the lower half of the case (the console being detached), the Great the upper, with the Pedal behind the main case.

> The general tonal layout of the organ derives mainly from English/American practices of the 18th and 19th centuries, but with additions and modifications intended to increase the organ's versatility so that both the liturgy and the broad spectrum of organ literature may be served. Some of the specific voices, such as the Stopped Diapason, would adhere to the still valid English tradition that flourished when the first two organs of St. Michael's were built. Although the basic specification is classical, the inclusion of a Celeste stop and several solo voices broadens the scope to include capabilities for music of the Romantic and Contemporary periods. We believe that the resulting instrument would adequately reflect its traditional roots without sacrificing in the least the versatility required of a modern liturgical organ.
>
> Charles Fisk to Rev. George A. Westerberg, June 19, 1972

The organ was dedicated in a morning service and Festal Evensong on February 2, 1975, followed by a series of five concerts held during the five following months. In the summer of 1983 the Pedal Mixture was replaced by a German Trumpet 8'.

Opus 70, 1976
First Presbyterian Church, Cazenovia, New York

Great (enclosed):		Choir (Rückpositiv):	
Stillgedackt	16'	Bourdon	8'
Prestant	8' (unenclosed)	Principal	4'
Chimney Flute	8' (wood)	Night Horn	4'
Gambe	8'	Nazard	$2\frac{2}{3}$'
Voix Céleste	8' (tenor C)	Prestant	2'
Octave	4'	Tierce	$1\frac{3}{5}$'
Wedge Flute	4' (open wood)	Larigot	$1\frac{1}{3}$'
Doublet	2'	Sharp	IV
Cornet	III	Cremona	8'
Mixture	IV–VI		
Trumpet	8'		
Hautboy	8'		

Pedal:	
Principal	16' (open wood)
Flute	8' (open metal)
Superoctave	4'
Bassoon	16'
Trumpet	8'

Couplers: Great/Choir, Choir/Great, Great/Pedal, Choir/Pedal
Tremulant, Cymbal Star
Balanced Swell Pedal (to Great)
Combinations: 5 General, 4 Great, 4 Choir, 3 Pedal, Cancel, Sforzando
Manual compass: 56 notes; Pedal compass: 30 notes
Wind pressure: $2\frac{1}{4}$"

Like the preceding organ, this instrument employs older casework (from a John G. Marklove organ) with matching new Rückpositiv and Pedal tower cases. It also has electrically controlled stop and combination action, and a detached console. The Great and Swell are combined into a single division, since space would not allow for three manual divisions. The 8' and 4' Great flutes, 8' Choir flute, and 16' and 4' Pedal principals are revoiced Marklove pipes.

The tonal design is by Charles Fisk and Robert Capen. It is unabashedly eclectic, the theory behind it being that an excellent church organ will result if only good placement, good voicing, and tracker key action are present. The Great division is in a Swell box, an unusual juxtaposition which gives flexibility for accompanying the choir and for performing certain pieces of the Romantic organ literature. Performance of this literature is also enhanced by certain softer stops included in the Great. Meanwhile, flexible winding—especially in the Choir division—makes for an authentically Baroque sound.

This organ is like no other. It has its own personality, its own pleasurable aspects, its own way of showing sadness or joy or anger. The exact nature of the instrument will be revealed only after much playing and much listening.

Charles Fisk, "From the Builder," dedication program, 1976

The organ was dedicated on May 16, 1976, with a morning service, followed by an afternoon recital by Robert Noehren.

Opus 71, 1977
First Congregational Church, Westfield, Massachusetts

Great:		Choir:	
Bourdon	16'	Stopt Diapason	8'
Prestant	8'	Spire Flute	4'
Chimney Flute	8'	Fifteenth	2'
Principal	4'	{ Nazard	$2^2/_3$'
Flute	4'	{ Sesquialtera	II
{ Night Horn	2'	Sharp	IV
{ Cornet	III	Clarinet	8'
{ Doublet	2'		
{ Mixture	V–VII		
Trumpet	8'		

Pedal:	
Principal	16'
(Octave	8')
(Superoctave	4')
Bassoon	16'

Couplers: Choir/Great, Choir/Pedal, Great/Pedal
Tremulant (Tremblant Doux)
Manual compass: 61 notes; Pedal compass: 32 notes
Wind pressure: $2^3/_4$"
Bracketed stops are double-drawing

Like the Cazenovia organ, this instrument employs some pipework from a previous much-rebuilt organ, originally built by Johnson & Son. This includes the Great 16' flute and Choir 8' flute, the manual reeds (entirely revoiced, with new tongues) and the metal 16' Principal in the Pedal. This latter stop, the bass of which was formerly in the façade, is mechanically unified using the Austin type of individual-valve action. This organ carried Charles Fisk's interest in Gottfried Silbermann's work a step further than any previous organ, particularly with regard to case design and layout.

> A year ago last spring I had an opportunity to see organs by the famous organ builder Gottfried Silbermann in East Germany... I was deeply impressed by the effectiveness of his smaller instruments, especially by the musical effectiveness of his organ cases. It occurred to me a week or two ago that your church might well be just the place for a case built to Silbermann's measurements. The result is what you see in the sketch, which, curiously enough, looks like cases built in America in the early 19th century, a decade or two before your present building was built. For this reason alone I believe this case will look fine in your church; it will certainly seem more at home than the more spare contemporary case with Pedal towers that we were planning for you earlier.
>
> Charles Fisk to Douglas Ward, November 8, 1975

The case design, with the Choir division placed in "Oberwerk" position above the Great, and the Pedal in back of all, found favor with the church. On the completion of the organ Fisk wrote:

> Our Opus 71 does not copy any Silbermann organ exactly, but it does employ one version of Silbermann's tone cabinet design for a two-manual organ, and its wind ducts, bellows and tremulant are to Silbermann's dimensions. The Silbermann organ most closely represented here is the 21-voice instrument at Grosshartmannsdorf near Freiberg, East Germany, an instrument of rare beauty.
>
> For Opus 71 we have used our own scales (pipe dimensions) rather than Silbermann's, although some of the voicing is after Silbermann's manner, most notably the 8' Prestant on the Great. The manual reeds, which would not have appeared in a Silbermann organ of this size, are from the Johnson organ and have their original shallots opened wide so as to produce something of the fiery reed sound known to Silbermann and Bach.
>
> The organ case façade is an adaptation of Silbermann's Grosshartmannsdorf pattern. The layout of the front pipes is Silbermann's, but the woodwork is greatly simplified. In this form the case resembles certain American organ cases of the early nineteenth century. The two ornamen-

tal gilded wave carvings atop the compartments were designed and carved by Ann Fisk, and are again an adaptation of a type used by Silbermann.

Charles Fisk, "From the Organ Builder," dedication program, 1977

The organ was dedicated on February 6, 1977 in a morning service, followed by an afternoon organ recital by Joan Lippincott.

Opus 72, 1981
Houghton Chapel, Wellesley College, Wellesley, Massachusetts

Oberwerk:		Rückpositiv:	
Quintadena	16'	Gedackt	8'
Principal	8'	Quintadena	8'
Spillpfeife	8'	Principal	4'
Octav	4'	Rohrflöte	4'
{ Octav	2'	Oktav	2'
{ Rauschpfeife	II	{ Nasat	3'
Mixtur	IV–VI	{ Sesquialter	II
Trompete	8'	Scharff	IV
		Trechterregal	8'
		Krummhorn	8'

Brustpositiv:		Pedal:	
Gedackt	8'	Subbass	16' (stopped wood)
Quintadena	4'	Posaune	16' (prepared for)
Waldflöte	2'	Spillpfeife	8' (from Oberwerk)
Doppelt Zimbel	II	Trompete	8' (from Oberwerk)
Regal	8'		
Schalmey	4'	Brustpedalia (prepared for)	

Couplers: Rückpositiv/Pedal, Rückpositiv/Oberwerk
Tremulant, Zimbelstern
Manual compass: 52 notes, CC, DD, EE–c_3, with subsemitones
Pedal compass: 25 notes, CC, DD, EE–d_1, with subsemitones
Wind pressure: 3¼"
Bracketed stops are double-drawing

Although the contract for this organ was signed in April of 1977, discussions between Charles Fisk and Owen Jander of Wellesley College had begun as early as 1972. It was from the beginning conceived of as a reconstruction or facsimile of a seventeenth-century North European organ, but as study for the project commenced and input was received from various quarters, the emphasis shifted from the Netherlandish type of organ known by Sweelinck to the North German type of instrument for which Scheidt, Scheidemann, Böhm, Lübeck, and Buxtehude wrote. This involved much study and several trips to Europe, during which Charles Fisk, aided by people such as Harald Vogel, Harry Hillebrand, Klaas Bolt, and Dirk Flentrop, was able to study pipework, casework, and other fragments of the work of Gottfried Fritzsche, his pupil Fritz Stellwagen, and others.

> Fritzsche brought *Lieblichkeit*—i.e., elegance—into the monumental art of organ building, and so brought the art to a level of excellence never perhaps equalled before or since.
>
> No intact Fritzsche organ remains. We do have, however, work from his pupils Stellwagen and Brunner, from his contemporary Esaius Compenius, and from his son H. C. Fritzsche, which, together with Praetorius's descriptions, should make it possible for us to reconstruct an organ in Fritzsche's style. My recent examinations of the organs in Tellingstedt, Altenbruch, and Lübeck in Germany, and Hillerød in Denmark, have given me the impetus I need. All that remains is to make certain detailed measurements...
>
> My feeling is that the time for building this organ is ripe. Although greater Boston is the center of organ culture in America, it has contracted for no major instrument since 1967, and has no significant instrument other than Wellesley's to look forward to. Furthermore, Wellesley's instrument will mark a huge stride in organ building practice, and is sure to contribute much to the understanding of how a large segment of the organ literature should be performed. This literature is of course *already* being performed on instruments we and others have built within the last dozen years, but it is being performed incorrectly due to the particular bias of these instruments. We badly need a new instrument to set our players aright. And we have *so many* good and promising players, who will instantly see the uses to which Wellesley's new organ may be put.
>
> Charles Fisk to Owen Jander, February 2, 1977

Funding problems delayed the beginning of construction, but Fisk's studies continued, and found application in other organs which were in progress. The completed design included casework based on that of the c. 1615 Fritzsche organ which Heinrich Schütz knew in the Dresden court chapel, human-powered bellows and a wind system based on measurements of period instruments, quarter-comma meantone tuning with subsemitones (split keys for D sharp/E flat and G sharp/A flat) in the three middle octaves, suspended action, and pipes meticulously scaled, constructed, and voiced to reproduce as faithfully as possible the sound of historic pipes such as those in the Stellwagen Brustwerk in the Jakobikirche of Lübeck. The pure meantone tuning and its refreshing effect on the music have been a revelation to many since the organ was completed, the builder included:

> We all knew we would learn from the experience, but no one of us would have guessed the extent. My own elation at discovering how a *new* organ built in the old style sounds when you tune it in quarter-comma meantone remains a lingering wonderment. Indeed, I am forced now to conclude that the organ reached its peak as a musical instrument during the meantone era, simply because its natural tendency to bind its tone into a single unity (by drawing) creates effects with purely tuned thirds and octave that we children of equal temperament impoverishment can never experience. I think, for example, that for us to have heard Reincken's 32′ instrument at the Katerinen in Hamburg, when it was in pure meantone, would have left us all agape.
>
> Charles Fisk to John Rowntree, May 17, 1982

The Wellesley organ was opened with a pair of identical concerts on October 2 and 4, 1981, given by Harald Vogel and members of the Musicalische Compagney. Shortly before the opening Charles Fisk, in an interview, commented on the musical effect of the organ and its influence on his work:

> Instruments of this period were *dance* instruments; they had the property of being able to move. When you move, *it* moves—unlike the great lumoxes of organs that were built in later periods that simply can't be made to give good reports of themselves.
>
> You do something in order to learn something. You produce the thing that will teach you what you want to learn; this has been an incredible opportunity. The organ in the Busch-Reisinger Museum at Harvard that was built in the late '30's was the second approximation in this country of an historical instrument. In 1958 they built a closer approximation. This new organ at Wellesley is another step in the process, and in time it will be found inadequate—that is, it will be overshadowed in the pedagogical sense, though not, I hope, in the musical. And I know that I cannot build an organ in the ways I did before because of the things I learned in building this one.
>
> Charles Fisk, in *The Boston Globe*, September 27, 1981

The "prepared-for" Pedal 16' reed stop was placed in the organ in 1984, and the carved pipe shades and Brustwerk door ornaments, funded separately, were completed in 1984 and 1985. The Brustpedalia division, to be located at either side of the keydesk, still awaits completion as of this writing. The organ is used regularly for recitals and seminars, and is the focal point of week-long seminars held annually in June by The Westfield Center for Early Keyboard Studies.

Opus 74, 1977
St. Peter's & St. Andrew's Church, Providence, Rhode Island

Manual:			Pedal:	
Prestant	8'		Subbass	16'
Gedackt	8'	(divided)		
Octave	4'			
Chimney Flute	4'	(divided)		
Fifteenth	2'	(divided)		
Twelfth	2⅔'	(bass)		
{ Nazard	2⅔'	(treble)		
{ Sesquialtera	II	(treble)		
Mixture	III–V			
Cromorne	8'	(divided)		

Coupler: Manual/Pedal
Tremulant, Cymbalstern
Machine stop affecting stops 2' and higher in pitch
Manual compass: 56 notes; Pedal compass: 30 notes
Divided stops divide at middle C

This small but versatile organ, built for a small liturgical church, bears a certain conscious visual resemblance to the central section of Opus 45, built in 1965:

> As you see, we have abandoned the idea of "boxes" because they really do not seem to work well under the window. They look stunted. The more animate case idea that we used at Christ Church, Westerly again seems to be the best for working around windows...
> It has a kind of swept wing wooden roof, curved and fitting the front pipe tops fairly closely, as you see. My belief is that all of the window will be visible if the viewer moves from one place to another, something that would not have been true with the other design. For accent we have

included a center tower of three pipes; from the Westerly organ we know that these have no obstructional effect whatever. The eye seems to see around such an element.

Charles Fisk to the Rev. Stuart Kent, March 29, 1976

The English influence can be observed here in the divided stops, the machine stop, and the general nature of the stoplist. But the Cromorne is forthrightly French in sound, and a last-minute gift by a church member made possible the first wind-driven Cymbelstern to appear in a Fisk organ (all previous ones having been electrically driven, usually by old 78 r.p.m. turntables).

This cheerful organ represents an effort to bring some of the ancient musical feeling of life into a small urban American church. Having but one manual keyboard, such an organ might be presumed to lack the vigor and resources of a larger church organ. This organ, however, tells us another story. Its sound is intended to be vigorous, youthful, pungent, and above all happy. For the sake of diversity, several stops... have been divided between B and middle C. This means that one hand can play on one voice (or melody) while the other can play on another voice (or accompaniment). In addition, there is a "machine stop" foot pedal for making quick changes of volume level; using this it is possible to imitate the effect of a two-manual organ.

Charles Fisk, in dedication program notes, 1977

The organ was dedicated on March 12, 1977, with two recitals. The afternoon recital was given by George Kent, assisted by violist Joseph Ceo; the evening recital by Frank Taylor, assisted by George Kent, trumpet.

Opus 75, 1977
North Carolina School of the Arts, Winston-Salem, North Carolina

Great:		Swell:	
Bourdon	16'	Violin Diapason	8'
Prestant	8'	Stopt Diapason (chimneys)	8'
Spire Flute	8'	Spitzflute	4'
Octave	4'	{ Quinta	1⅓'
Flute	2'	Cornet	III–IV
Superoctave	2'	{ Fifteenth	2'
Cornet	II	Fourniture	III
Mixture	IV–VI	Trumpet	8'
Trumpet	8'	Hautbois	8'
Voix Humaine	8'		
Clarion	4'		

Choir:		Pedal:	
Gedackt	8'	Prestant (open wood)	16'
Prestant	4'	Octave	8'
Chimney Flute	4'	{ Superoctave	4'
Doublet	2'	Mixture	IV
{ Nazard	2⅔'	Bassoon	16'
Sesquialter	III	Trumpet	8'
Sharp	IV	Shawm	4'
Cromorne	8'		

Couplers: Swell/Choir, Choir/Great, Great/Pedal, Swell/Pedal, Choir/Pedal
Tremblant Doux (Great)
Wind Stabilizer (activates concussion bellows)
Balanced Swell Pedal
Manual compass: 56 notes; Pedal compass: 30 notes
Wind Pressure: 2¼" to manuals; 2⅝" to Pedal
Bracketed stops are double-drawing; the two Great 2' stops are also on a double-drawing knob which provides one or the other, but not both together.

This is the second Fisk organ in which the case shape, wind system, and general layout were derived from the practices of Gottfried Silbermann, although this case, unlike the Westfield one, is contemporary in appearance. Several other trends come to focus in this instrument. It was the first in which a significant portion of the pipework was of hammered lead, and the third to have suspended key action.

> Suspended action is the most direct possible in that there are no squares between the roller board and the key. The balanced key action we have heretofore been using employs two sets of squares, and while these add the minimum of friction, they perhaps are not the last word. We used suspended action in the Baltimore Great organ years ago, and more recently at the University of Vermont, where it is clear that the suspended action is responsible for a different, and probably more musical, feel to the touch.
>
> Charles Fisk to John Mueller, November 19, 1975

As this organ is the school's main teaching and recital organ, its specification is unabashedly eclectic, containing elements of North and Central German styles as well as the French. The Trumpet and Hautbois in the Swell, for example, are based on Cavaillé-Coll practices, while the Voix Humaine in the Great derives from the small Clicquot organ in Houdan. The Swell box itself is rather ingeniously fitted into the physical scheme, and its shutters are directed toward the ceiling.

> The organ itself seems remarkable. Some of this must be Mr. G. Silbermann's magic, since we copied his layout and wind system. The sound is sort of "shock mounted," "cushioned on air," or just in general seems to be embedded in a big bowl of exactly the right flavor of Jello. In any case the "give" in the wind (resonance about 2 per second) takes away most of the hardness that characterizes so much that has seemed a compulsory part of modern organ building. Meanwhile, the big, loose case fitted up to the backwall seems perfect. Don't ask me why.
>
> Charles Fisk to Dr. Robert Newman, July 13, 1977

The organ was inaugurated with a weekend of concerts in 1977. On December 2 the NCSA Orchestra and Chamber Choir gave a program of concerted music under the direction of Nicholas Harsanyi, followed by a recital by John S. Mueller on December 3, and an Alumni Organ Concert on December 4.

DUKE UNIVERSITY, DURHAM, NORTH CAROLINA: Opus 76, 1978

Opus 76A, 1978
Westminster Choir College, Princeton, New Jersey

Great:		Positive:	
Spire Flute	8' (prestant)	Gedackt	8'
Principal	4'	Chimney Flute	4'
{ Doublet	2'	{ Nazard	2⅔'
{ Fourniture	III	{ Cornet	III
Cromorne	8'	{ Octave	2'
		{ Mixture	II (2' & 1⅓')

Pedal:	
Subbass	16'
Bourdon	8'
Octave	4'

Couplers: Great/Pedal, Positive/Pedal, Positive/Great
Tremulant
Manual compass: 56 notes; Pedal compass: 30 notes
Bracketed stops are double-drawing

These two organs were a pair of "twins," built at the same time and to all intents and purposes identical, although the Duke instrument had a flat pedalboard while the pedalboard of the Westminster organ was concave and radiating; the Duke organ was also voiced somewhat more softly, due to its location in a smaller room.

The following comments were made by Charles Fisk in response to some questions from a Westminster faculty member:

> I too wish we could do better on our double drawing stop action. It's very clumsy, and the main reason for doing it is to talk myself into making the organ bigger for the same price. Cutting down the size of the stop action and the number of stop knobs saves money in a number of ways, of course.
>
> Part of the trick with the wind (I vaguely suspect) is Silbermann's way of subdividing wind boxes (pallet boxes). Even on a little division he seldom used a single chest, but two instead. He may have felt that the more twigs there are on the wind tree, the less you could sense anything simple in their aggregate motion. As you know, I divided the pallet box at Westminster in two by way of following this rule, if that's what it is.
>
> Charles Fisk to Mark Brombaugh, May 23, 1978

The Westminster organ was opened with a recital by organ department chairperson Joan Lippincott on November 27, 1978.

Opus 78, 1979
House of Hope Presbyterian Church, St. Paul, Minnesota

Great:		Swell:	
Prestant	16'	Stillgedackt	16'
Octave	8'	Diapason	8'
Gambe	8'	Viola da Gamba	8'
Flûte Harmonique	8'	Voix Céleste	8'
Bourdon	8'	Chimney Flute	8'
Octave	4'	Italian Principal	4'
Rohrflöte	4'	{ Quinta	2⅔'
Superoctave	2'	Sesquialter	II
{ Grave Mixture	II	{ Fifteenth	2'
Cornet	V	Fourniture	IV–VI
Mixture	VIII–XII	Contra Hautboy	16'
Double Trumpet	16'	Trumpet	8'
German Trumpet	8'	Oboe	8'
French Trumpet	8'	Clarion	4'
Orlos	4' (I–III)		

Rückpositiv:		Brustwerk:	
Holzquintadehn	16'	Gedackt	8'
Prestant	8'	Quintadena	4'
Bourdon	8'	Waldflöte	2'
Octave	4'	{ Tierce	1⅗'
Baarpijp	4'	Echo Cornet	III
Grosse Tierce	3⅕'	{ Quinta	1⅓'
{ Nazard	2⅔'	Cymbal	III
Sesquialtera	II	Regal	8'
Night Horn	2'	Schalmey	4'
Doublet	2'		
Sharp	V–VIII		
Dulcian	16'		
Trechterregal	8'		
Cromorne	8'		

Pedal:
Contra Bourdon	32' (electric action)
Prestant	16'
Subbass	16' (extension of 32')
Octave	8'
Gedackt	8'
Superoctave	4'
Mixture	V
Contra Bassoon	32'
Trombone	16'
Cornopean	8'
Shawm	4'

Couplers: Swell/Great, Rückpositiv/Great, Brustwerk/Great, Swell/Rückpositiv, Great/Pedal, Rückpositiv/Pedal, Swell/Pedal, Brustwerk/Pedal
General Tremulant, Tremblant Doux, General Wind Stabilizer, Rückpositiv Wind Stabilizer, Balanced Swell Pedal
Composition Pedals (reversible): Great Flue Chorus, Great Reed Chorus, Swell Forte Stops
Ventil Pedals: Great Windchest, Pedal Reeds, Pedal Flues (excluding 32' and 16' Bourdons)
Manual compass: 56 notes; Pedal compass: 30 notes
Wind Pressure: 3½"

This instrument was the largest to be built by Charles Fisk. In it many trends, ideas, and recent lessons converged to make it an eclectic instrument of a very unique sort. Pipe scales from the Silbermann brothers coexist with a Brustwerk which, like that of the Wellesley organ which was to follow, was based on a seventeenth-century North German model. French and German Trumpets stand side by side; Gambas and Flûtes Harmoniques after Cavaillé-Coll make possible a true French Romantic sound.

> During the past year or so, whenever I have contemplated the instrument and its possibilities, I have realized more and more that this organ is asking to be the major work of my lifetime.
> Considering that I probably have not more than twenty years left for building organs, and that one quarter of that period is already contracted for, I am the more anxious that House of Hope become our *pièce de résistance*.
> Recent trips to France and Germany have let me see more clearly how we might synthesize a design that really will accomplish the "unattainable" ideal of playing *all* literature well. Therefore, I enclose herewith a

new specification for the House of Hope organ which I hope will not be out of reach, even though it is somewhat more expensive than the original one.

Charles Fisk to Sharon Kleckner, February 22, 1977

The organ was installed in the spacious rear gallery of the church, whose initially poor acoustics had been substantially improved prior to the installation. The inaugural recital was given by Daniel Chorzempa on November 18, 1979. This was followed by a series of concerts over the following six months by Joan Lippincott (who performed *Epiphanies*, a newly commissioned work by Daniel Pinkham), Fenner Douglass, and Nancy Lancaster which culminated in the first House of Hope Organ Institute in June. In the summer of 1980 a major recital was given at House of Hope Church by David Craighead during a national convention of the American Guild of Organists. Craighead, in planning his program, requested a description of the organ, and Charles Fisk responded with the following commentary:

> This organ has the *purpose* of playing all music. To do this it leans in three directions at once: 17th century German, 18th century French, 19th century French. Cavaillé-Coll is drawn from in the Gt. Foundations (Harmonic Flute 8, Gambe 8, Bourdon 8 and to some extent the 8' Open, also Sw. Gambe and Céleste, Hautbois, Basson 16', Trompette 8' and Clairon 4'). These elements are really copies from Cavaillé-Coll and are curious—for example, the strings are not beautiful in the American sense but have that gently nasal quality that we think of as somehow French—this being achieved by using brass bridges instead of ears and rollerbeards. Curiously like the scraping of a real gamba! Haven't heard the Swell reeds yet but I don't expect them to be truly unleashed—rather to be restrained in Cavaillé-Coll's manner (which isn't all that restrained). The Great reeds are different from the Swell reeds and divide into two camps: 1. The 16' and 8' German style trumpets with leathered lead-faced shallots (the style developed by the Scherers in 1580 or so) which sound like E. M. Skinner Trombas (!) but are much quicker, and thus work in the true German ensemble, and 2. The 8' and 4' French reeds which will be loud and brassy as I can make them. The latter are straight from Dom Bedos and therefore should make the best Grand Jeu we've ever constructed. Clarion incidentally increases to three ranks in the treble, in order to compensate for the natural weakness of reed trebles. These French reeds were really strong in the shop and I hope they end up being the right kind of sensation here. In other words, I hope they are more treat than treatment! The Great fluework is generally broad and unflinching. The 16' and 8' Prestants will be full and deep in their sound—as dignified and estimable as I can make them. These are of 70% tin. The interior chorus

work (Octave, 12th, 15th) are of hammered lead and therefore carry a lot of weight without shrillness. The large mixture (VIII–XII) is all of the same (narrow) scale but ⅓ of the pipes are hammered spotted metal and ⅔ are hammered lead, the object being to combine weight and shimmer in the same stop. This seems to work out well. The Great Flutes 8 and 4 are of lead, large and gentle, Great Cornet V is from c_1 and is quite strong.

None of the Rückpositiv is working yet except a couple of foundations, but basically it is a small Great, with 8′ Prestant of tin and 16′ wooden Quintadena (Holzquintadehn). The Rp. case is very low (you can almost touch the bottom of it from the nave center aisle below), so it may scald the necks of the parishioners right underneath when fully drawn. I don't expect to hold back the Rp. reeds or upperwork, so it should be formidable. Again, the reeds are split into pure French and pure German. Cromorne 8′ is an enormous French Cromorne (Dom Bedos's No. 1 scale, looks like an anti-tank device) while Dulzian 16′ and Trechterregal 8′ are gentle and controlled copies of 17th-century German work, leathered lead-faced shallots and all. Gross Tierce 3⅕′ is designed to go with the 16′ flue. The Sesquialtera is flute scale and is the logical place for playing the tierce-entaille.

Brustwerk is a close copy of the Brustwerk of Stellwagen at the Jakobikirche in Luebeck. Not only the stops but the chest layout and dimensions are copied. The only additions are the Cornet, which is fairly strong and somewhat narrow in scale, and the Larigot (Quint) that goes with the Cymbal. All is hammered lead. This division really sounds old, like a throwback. Because we copied Stellwagen's pallet box and duct sizes the wind is somewhat fluttery on the Brust . . . which seems very appropriate. The 8′ Regal and 4′ Schalmey are dead copies of Stellwagen and sound it. If you want to play your Compenius orgletmuzik, this is the place. But don't get me wrong—this little division has fighting ways!

The Pedal is in towers widely separated to make room for the choir. Bourdon 32′ and 16′ is an electro-pneumatic unit from the old organ (!), large scale. Front pipes are 70% tin, Pedal 16′ Open, not small. All Pedal fluework is large scale—no lack of bass at all. Mixture has 5⅓′ in it. 32′ reed is half length cylindrical, a large clarinet not weak like Harvard. Trombone 16′ is of wood and has leathered shallots (German) which make it smooth, quick and a bit ponderous. 8′ Trumpet is a massive German stop, quick, leathered, strong but *not* full of high overtones. Clarion 4′ is a very large French Trumpet, very strong; can be used an octave lower for Cantus in French Plein Jeux.

All normal couplers exist. Manual sequence is 1. Rugwerk, 2. Great, 3. Swell, 4. Brust. Straight pedal board, but pedal spacing is about like an American concave-radiating ped. bd.—you won't want to use quite as much heel as usual. Temperament is watered-down Werckmeister II. The F chord is quite smooth, but I tried to keep the black keys from sounding as raw as in Werckmeister.

Charles Fisk to David Craighead, April 4, 1979

Opus 79, 1980
First Presbyterian Church, Charleston, West Virginia

Great:			Swell:	
Prestant	16′		Bourdon	16′
Octave	8′		Geigen	8′
Gambe	8′		Stillgedackt	8′
Flûte Harmonique	8′		Voce Umano	8′
Chimney Flute	8′		Italian Principal	4′
Octave	4′		{ Nazard	2⅔′
{ Waldflöte	4′		{ Sesquialtera	II
{ Cornet	IV		Flageolet	2′
{ Doublet	2′		{ Fifteenth	2′
{ Mixture	VI–VIII		{ Fourniture	IV
Trumpet	8′		Bassoon	16′
Clarion	4′		Trumpet	8′
			Hautboy	8′

Positive:			Pedal:	
Bourdon	8′		Prestant	16′
Prestant	4′		Bourdon	16′
Night Horn	4′		Baarpijp	8′
{ Nasat	2⅔′		{ Superoctave	4′
{ Sesquialter	II		{ Mixture	IV
{ Sifflet	1′		Trombone	16′
{ Quartane	II		Trumpet	8′
{ Doublet	2′			
{ Sharp	V			
Cromorne	8′			

Couplers: Swell/Great, Positive/Great, Swell/Positive, Great/Pedal, Swell/Pedal, Positive/Pedal
Tremulant, Wind Stabilizer, Balanced Swell Pedal
Two adjustable pairs of combination pedals; one for Great/Pedal, the other for Positive/Swell
Manual compass: 56 notes; Pedal compass: 30 notes
Bracketed stops are double-drawing

This organ shares many design features with the St. Paul and Rochester instruments, but is unique in that it makes functional use of a handsome case front which was originally designed as mere "stage dressing" for an organ chamber in Harvard University's Memorial Church. In storage in various places since 1966, the case front eventually was separated from the rest of the organ and became available in 1978. Charles Fisk saw its possibilities for the Charleston organ and acquired it.

> The case for this organ was built in 1931 for Appleton Chapel at Memorial Church, Harvard University, by Irving and Casson of Cambridge, Massachusetts, a famous woodworking firm which at one time employed as many as one hundred wood carvers. The design was derived from the case of an organ by George England (1765) for St. Stephen's Church, Walbrook, London, designed by Sir Christopher Wren. The original front pipes were made by Hook & Hastings. The case pipes did not speak (these do) and were each of the same diameter (these aren't). Behind the case from 1932 to 1966 stood a 100-stop Aeolian-Skinner organ.
>
> By combining the casework, patterned after an 18th century case, and an 18th century-style organ, we believe the case has achieved a new integrity.
>
> Charles Fisk, in dedication brochure, 1980

Although a contract had been drawn up with the church in 1975, a change in location from front to rear gallery and the decision to utilize the old Harvard case front prompted a thorough re-thinking of the tonal and physical design:

> I have made some alterations which will be of special interest to you. The addition of the 16' Open to the Great will add gravity to the plenum as befits a building the size of yours, while the shifting of the Great bourdon 16' to the Swell will do likewise for the full Swell—in short, the organ will sound bigger than it would have with the old specification. Further, the addition of the Gambe and the Flûte Harmonique to the Great yields the "Fonds de huit" which is so beautiful in a large building and so helpful in the performance of 19th century French organ music, not to mention ordinary anthem accompaniments. The French "jeu de tierce" has moved from the Positive to the Swell, leaving the Positive to become an Oberwerk in the style of Gottfried Silbermann, with the fanciful narrow-scaled mutations he knew so well how to build. The appearance of both 16 foot flues on the Pedal should add to the Pedal's capabilities for accompaniment.
>
> Charles Fisk to David Deaderick, September 20, 1978

The organ was dedicated the morning of October 12, 1980; an inaugural recital by Fenner Douglass was given in the afternoon.

Opus 80, 1981
Storrs Congregational Church, Storrs, Connecticut

Great:		Swell:	
Bourdon	16'	Geigen Diapason	8'
Prestant	8'	Voix Céleste	8'
Spire Flute	8'	Gedackt	8'
Octave	4'	Spitzflöte	4'
{ Doublet	2'	{ Fifteenth	2'
{ Mixture	V–VII	{ Sesquialtera	III
{ Blockflöte	4'	{ Quinta	1⅓'
{ Cornet (4 ranks begin at middle C)	V	{ Fourniture	IV
		Dulcian	16'
Trumpet	8'	Trumpet	8'
Clarion	4'	Oboe	8'
Choir (Rückpositiv):		Pedal:	
Stopt Diapason	8'	Subbass (lowest 8 pipes from Great)	16'
Prestant	4'		
Night Horn	4'	Baarpijp	8'
{ Nazard	2⅔'	{ Superoctave	4'
{ Cornet	II	{ Mixture	IV
{ Doublet	2'	Trombone	16'
{ Sharp	V	Trumpet	8'
Cromorne	8'		

Couplers (drawknob): Swell/Great, Choir/Great, Swell/Choir
Couplers (pedal): Great/Pedal, Swell/Pedal, Choir/Pedal
Tremulant, Wind Stabilizer, Balanced Swell Pedal
Manual compass: 61 notes; Pedal compass: 32 notes
Wind Pressure: 2¼"
Bracketed stops are double-drawing

When this church's organ committee was visiting the work of prospective builders, the organ which made the most lasting impression on them was that in Boston's Old West Church (Opus 55). This, plus the similarity of the church's architectural style to that of the older meetinghouse, resulted in an instrument which has a closer relationship to the earlier organ, both tonally and visually, than most of the intervening work. Like the Old West organ, it also contains some revoiced older pipework which includes the Pedal reeds, the Swell 8' reeds, the Great 4' Clarion, the Swell 8' flues, and some Pedal fluework.

In his later years, E. Power Biggs was heard to comment that, historically, there must be at least a dozen ways in which to build a truly perfect organ. Today's organ builder, finding himself both fascinated and perplexed by the choices that organ history seems to thrust upon him, must search for boundary conditions that will help him determine the character of any instrument he is to build. For our new organ at the Storrs Congregational Church, it is perhaps interesting to see how boundary conditions brought about the final design of the instrument.

First, at Storrs, comes the need to accompany the congregational singing; next, the need for accompaniment for the choir; then comes the need for organ voluntaries, i.e, preludes, postludes, and recital music. Beyond lies the fact that Storrs is a seat of higher learning, meaning that the organ should be proper for the teaching of college students. A further consideration is the nature of the other organs in the immediate area, because the popular understanding of what an organ can or should be depends on the aesthetic summum bonum of the instruments readily available for hearing. Implicit here, though seldom stated, is the idea that a church and its organ comprise more than just a spiritual haven; they are ideally a vital means of instruction and enlightenment for the entire community.

Physical boundary conditions also have their say. The congregation of this church has never had need for a large, lofty building—hence no chance for reverberant cathedral acoustics that can make an average organ sound superb. Placing the organ in the rear gallery has made possible a directness and vitality of pipe speech that compensates somewhat for the lack of reverberation in the acoustics. It is greatly to be hoped, of course, that future alterations to the building will include minimizing the amount of carpeting on the floor, since carpet has such a damping effect on reverberation.

The gallery ceiling happens to be just high enough to accommodate a full-length 8 foot pipe; this determines the length of the longest pipes in both the Great and the Pedal divisions. These pipes are to be seen in the main case, the large copper pipes at the sides belonging to the Pedal, those of hammered lead and spotted metal nearer the center belonging to the Great. A detached keydesk, although making the tracker action less agile, serves the dual purpose of providing space for the Swell division and facilitating the organist's task of directing the choir while playing. The Rückpositiv cabinet makes an attractive and traditional centerpiece for the gallery railing and acts as a musical foil for the Great.

The Storrs Congregational Church building was clearly intended to emulate the best of early 19th century New England church architecture. In those days the best organs came from the Boston builders, William Goodrich, Thomas Appleton, and E. & G. G. Hook, and would have been lovely pieces of mahogany furniture adorning the church gallery. Our choice of mahogany and our use of traditional shapes, especially those taken from the fine arches in the gallery windows, is an effort to recapture some of the grace of an early Boston organ.

An effort has been made to make possible the performance of all schools of organ music. The Great and Positive reeds are French, the Swell Trumpet and Oboe are English, and the Swell Dulcian and Pedal Trombone are essentially German. Cornets in the French style (Great and Choir) and in the German style (Swell) are included. Although the *plena* are from the 18th century, the Swell division, complete with strings, makes possible much of the romantic literature. Eighteenth century flexible winding can be stabilized to 20th century standards by the drawing of a knob. And three manuals instead of two yields not only diversity in performance but the possibility of teaching students the intricacies of music for a large organ.

Charles Fisk, in dedication brochure, 1981

The organ was dedicated with a two-day program which included a lecture by Fenner Douglass and a recital by Fisk employees on November 21, 1981, followed by a morning dedication service and afternoon recital by Douglass on November 22.

Opus 82, 1982
Christ United Methodist Church, Greensboro, North Carolina

Great:		Swell:	
Montre	16'	Gambe	8'
Prestant	8'	Voix Céleste	8'
Flûte Harmonique	8'	Bourdon	8'
Spire Flute	8'	Flûte Traversière	8'
Octave	4'	Flûte Conique	4'
{ Waldflöte	4'	{ Doublette	2'
{ Cornet	V	{ Cornet	III
Octave	2'	Trompette	8'
Blockflute	2'	Hautbois	8'
Mixture	VI–XI	Voix Humaine	8'
Doublet Trumpet	16'		
German Trumpet	8'		
{ French Trumpet	8'		
{ Grand Jeu	II		

Positiv:		Pedal:	
Bourdon	16'	⎰ Bourdon	16'
Prestant	8'	⎱ Bourdon	16' & 32'
Chimney Flute	8'	Montre	16'
Octave	4'	Baarpijp	8'
Night Horn	4'	⎰ Superoctave	4'
⎰ Nazard	2⅔'	⎱ Mixture	V
⎱ Sesquialtera	II	Trombone	16'
⎰ Fifteenth	2'	Trumpet	8'
⎱ Mixture	IV–VI		
Dulcian	16'		
Cromorne	8'		

Couplers: Swell/Positiv, Swell/Great, Positiv/Great, Swell/Pedal, Positiv/Pedal, Great/Pedal
Tremulant/Tremblant Doux (double draw)
Appel (Swell), Wind Stabilizer, Balanced Swell Pedal
Manual compass: 56 notes; Pedal compass: 30 notes
Wind Pressure: 3¼"
Bracketed stops are double-drawing

While the stoplist of this organ is indicative of strong Classic/Romantic French influences, the inclusion of German Baroque reeds and other elements makes this a broadly eclectic instrument. The room is favorable to bass frequencies, and the gift by Professor Harold Andrews of the lowest twelve notes of the 32' Bourdon was therefore a useful addition to the tonal scheme. The height of the room allowed for a 16' Principal, and its design allowed for an elegantly contemporary case.

> Although I have gone no further than to imagine it in my own mind, I see the organ case as a rather free standing, asymmetrical cabinet of oak wood complete with display pipes in various forms, including horizontal trumpets "en chamade." This cabinet would stand on its own pedestal, or trunk, situated in the forward-most section of the present choir area, and it would rise to a point close to the ceiling. Like a free form sculpture or piece of furniture it would not appear to be connected to any wall, nor would it appear to be parallel to any wall. It would be an element free of the building, yet designed in close relation to it. In my opinion it would add the finishing visual touch to your sanctuary. Musically there would be nothing like it in your area.
>
> Charles Fisk to Calvin Michaels, November 18, 1975

Although the final form of the organ case was symmetrical, and it did not contain horizontal reeds, it unquestionably embodies the spirit of Charles Fisk's early conceptualization.

> Opus 82, the organ we have just completed for Christ United Methodist Church in Greensboro, like all our instruments, is singular in its concept and execution. This church is larger and loftier than the churches we are normally privileged to work in; such spaciousness suggested to us that a tall instrument standing clear and free in the right front corner would be a welcome center of attention matching the existing centers of worship table and pulpit. The usefulness and closely knit character of the congregation suggested, too, that the organ should speak its mind with vigor.
>
> Tonally, we have built an organ that has no great number of stops but that makes exceptionally efficient use of those it has. The breadth of knowledge about organ and organ music that currently pervades North Carolina's rich musical life has led us to provide the broadest historical pallette of colors available resources would allow. Among these are a complete *Grand Jeu* and *Petit Jeu* for classical French music, complete flue and reed chorus in classical German style, a Swell division typical of a nineteenth century French organ of moderate size, flutes of all kinds, and—perhaps most important of all—the gravity and nobility that comes from open 8' pipes on the Positive, open 16' pipes on the Great, and stopped 32' pipes on the Pedal. Polished copper was chosen for the largest open pipes as much for its musical excellence as for the warm visual quality it lends to the church's lovely brick interior.
>
> Charles Fisk, in dedication brochure, 1982

This organ was opened on October 17, 1982, with a morning worship service, followed by afternoon and evening recitals played by David Craighead.

Opus 83, 1983
Downtown United Presbyterian Church, Rochester, New York

Great:
    Prestant   16'
    Principal   8'
    Spire Flute   8'
    Flûte Harmonique   8'
    Octave   4'
    { Flute   4'
      Cornet   V (from Middle C)
    { Superoctave   2'
      Mixture   VI–VIII
    Trumpet   8'
    Clarion   4'

Swell:
    Gambe   8'
    Voix Céleste   8'
    Cor de Nuit   8'
    Italian Principal   4'
    Quinta $1\frac{1}{3}'$
    { Waldflöte   2'
      Fourniture   IV
    Basson   16'
    Trompette   8'
    Hautbois   8'

Positive:
    Prestant   8'
    Bourdon   8'
    Octave   4'
    Baarpijp   4'
    { Nazard $2\frac{2}{3}'$
      Sesquialtera   II
    Doublet   2'
    Mixture   IV–VI
    Cromorne   8'
    Trechterregal   8'

Pedal:
    Prestant   16'
    { Bourdon   16'
      Bourdon   16' & 32'
    Octave   8'
    { Superoctave   4'
      Mixture   IV
    Trombone   16'
    Trumpet   8'

Couplers: Swell/Positive, Swell/Great, Positive/Great, Swell/Pedal, Positive/Pedal, Great/Pedal
Tremulant, Wind Stabilizer, Great to Pedal Reversible
Manual compass: 56 notes; Pedal compass: 30 notes
Wind Pressure: $3\frac{1}{4}''$
Bracketed stops are double-drawing

This organ, in its carefully thought out eclecticism, shares a common concept with the earlier instruments in St. Paul, Charleston, and Greensboro; like the University of Vermont organ its case incorporates a "suspended" Positive division, although in this instance it serves as a screen for the shutters of the Swell division immediately behind it. In a letter to Eastman student Mark Coffey, written in July 1982, Charles Fisk stated that his object in building organs like the Rochester instrument was "to change the definition of the word *organ*."

A few flutes, strings, and reeds from a previous organ were revoiced and incorporated into the new instrument, largely in the Swell and Pedal (and including the 32′ stop). Initially it was planned to place the organ in a rear gallery, but concern about the gallery's weight-bearing properties led to a reevaluation and the bold decision by the church to locate the organ in front of the former chancel, which then became a chapel.

> Our original intent was to stand the new organ in the large rear gallery of the church, leaving the front of the church . . . pretty much unchanged. As the organ's designer, I would not have presumed to suggest a more drastic change, because I know and understand so well how people come to love their church the way it is.
>
> But to my utter surprise, when it came time to think seriously about how we were to build this organ, a totally new idea (of which I highly approved) was put forward by the church. It involved using the organ to divide off the chancel into a kind of chapel and bringing the chancel forward of the proscenium arch as if by way of bringing the holiest part of the church directly into the midst of the congregation. Acoustically, of course, this meant that all of the sources of sound—the minister, the choir, and the organ—suddenly achieved a hitherto unknown presence for the listener, especially beneficial for music because no sound need be forced in its effect. But I confess that what truly amazed me most was the total architectural change wrought in the building interior. Thanks to the vision of Frank Grosso and others, there is an openness and lightness of spirit now precisely expressed, a spirit that has great meaning for me, personally. Were I a citizen of Rochester, I would feel very much like joining this church because of the workings of the spirit that I know can and will take place within these walls.
>
> Charles Fisk, in dedication booklet, 1983

The dedication of this organ was celebrated with a full day of activities which included a morning dedication service, three afternoon lectures given by W. Thomas Smith, Steven Dieck and Robert Cornell, and Prof. Russell Saunders, plus an evening concert by J. Melvin Butler and the church's choir.

Opus 84, 1984
Abbey Chapel, Mt. Holyoke College, South Hadley, Massachusetts

Great:		Rückpositiv:	
Prestant	16'	{ Gedackt	8'
Octava	8'	{ Gedackt (treble, open)	II
Spillpfeife	8'	Quintadena	8'
Violon	8'	Prestant	4'
Octava	4'	Rohrflöte	4'
Offenflöte	4'	{ Nazard	2⅔'
{ Twelfth	2⅔'	{ Cornet	II
{ Sesquialtera	1⅗'	Waldflöte	2'
Superoctava	2'	Cimbel	IV
Quinta	1⅓'	Dulcian	16'
Mixture	II	Shawn	8'
Sifflet	⅔'		
Scharff	II		
Trumpet	8'		

Pedal:
    Open Bass   (wood) 16'
    Spillpfeife (from Great) 8'
    Choralbass   4'
    Posaune   16'
    Trumpet (from Great) 8'

Couplers: Rückpositiv/Great (shove coupler), Great/Pedal, Rückpositiv/Pedal
Tremulant, Zimbelstern, Nachtigal, Glockenspiel, Tympani
Compasses: Great, 58 notes; Rückpositiv, 56 notes; Pedal, 30 notes
Wind Pressure: 1¾"
Bracketed stops are double-drawing

The design and placement of this organ underwent many transformations during the period of its planning and design. At first it was thought to place it at the front of the chapel, and to make it an eclectic instrument of three manuals; later it was agreed that it should be in the rear gallery, and a more Silbermann-inspired design was considered. With the coming of a new college organist, Margaret Irwin-Brandon, the emphasis again changed, this time to an instrument with an Italian bias:

> Since Meg's particular interest is the Renaissance Italian organ, and since Mt. Holyoke's chapel will presumably retain the services of the Skinner organ, it has seemed to me that the idea of building an Italian style instrument could well be a good one, although I have never seen an early Italian instrument and would have to teach myself how to build one. I would never undertake such a project, of course, if I had not had such success in building an organ in early German style for Wellesley College.
>
> Charles Fisk to Carl Weinrich, December 29, 1981

Although a planned visit to Italy did not materialize, Fisk began to research Italian pipe scales. Meanwhile, delays caused by acoustical improvement of the chapel and the indecisions concerning the style and placement of the organ had caused Opus 85 to be begun before Opus 84, and during the additional planning time which this allowed, the Mount Holyoke organ evolved into an eclectic instrument of a very different kind—a synthesis of Renaissance elements both Italian and German, housed in a Gothic main case with a Renaissance Rückpositiv. Along with this design the gallery placement also evolved into a European double-gallery arrangement, with the organ lofted close to the ceiling. Fisk worked closely with the architects in integrating the design of the new upper gallery with that of the organ, and his ideas were largely carried out:

> Always in the old churches the organ was supported on a wooden gallery made of large timbers. I don't know how much it would cost, but the music and the visual effect would be fine if we could have a wooden gallery with dark stained 6 x 6's for joists, with no ceiling underneath—sort of barn construction. An open wooden structure under the organ will resonate when the organ is played full, something like the soundboard of a violin or piano.
>
> Charles Fisk to Wayne Gass, February 18, 1982

The completed organ is unique in many ways. Its low wind pressure gives it a sound which is gentler than that of some of the organs immediately preceding it, but because of its placement it projects unusually well. The fifth-comma meantone tuning makes it ideal for Renaissance music, but compatible with later music as well. The organ dedication weekend, February 15–17, 1985, included lectures, a performance of Handel's *Ode for St. Cecilia's Day*, a festival service, a recital by Mireille Lagacé, and a program of chamber music with organ.

Opus 85, 1984
Stanford University Chapel, Stanford, California

Great:		Rückpositiv:	
Prestant	16'	Prestant	8'
Quintadehn	16'	Gedackt	8'
Octava	8'	Quintadehn	8'
Spillpfeife	8'	Octava	4'
Violon	8'	Rohrflöte	4'
Quinta	5⅓'	{ Quinta	2⅔'
Octava	4'	{ Sesquialter	II
Super Octava	2'	{ Super Octava	2'
{ Quinta	2⅔'	{ Mixture	IV-VIII
{ Cornet	III	Dulcian	16'
Mixture	VIII-XIV	Cromorne	8'
Trommeten	16'	Trechterregal	8'
Trommeten	8'		
Trompette	8'		
Clarion	4' (II)		

Seitenwerk:		Brustpositiv:	
Principal Schweigel	8'	Gedackt	8'
Rohrflöte	8'	Quintadehn	4'
Holzoctava	4'	Waldflöte	2'
{ Doublette	2'	Doppelt Cimbel	II
{ Cornet	III	Regal	8'
{ Sifflöte	1'	Schalmey	4'
{ Mixture	IV		
Vox Humana	8'		

Pedal:		Brustpedalia:	
Prestant	16' (from Great)	Jungfrauenregal	4'
{ Subbass	16'	Cornett	2'
{ Contra Bourdon	32'	Bauernflöte	1'
Quintadehn	16' (from Great)		
Octava	8' (from Great)		
Spillpfeife	8' (from Great)		
Violon	8' (from Great)		
Octava	4' (from Great)		
Superoctava	2' (from Great)		
Contraposaune	32'		
Posaune	16'		
Trompete	8'		
Trommeten	8' (from Great)		
Trompette	8' (from Great)		
Clarion	4' (II, from Great)		

Couplers: Rückpositiv/Great, Seitenwerk/Great, Rückpositiv/Pedal, Great/Pedal
Tremulant, Wind Stabilizer
Prepared for: Cimbelstern, Nachtigal, Glockenspiel
Compasses: Great, Rückpositiv, Seitenwerk, 54 notes; Brustpositiv, 52 notes; Pedal, 30 notes
Bracketed stops are double-drawing

Yet another form of eclecticism shapes the tonal design of this unusual organ. Since the chapel's large Murray Harris organ serves the needs of Romantic music, the Fisk organ combines elements from the Renaissance and Baroque—North German, Central German, and French. The Brustpositiv is drawn from the same Stellwagen model as the Brustwerks in St. Paul and Wellesley, and the Brustpedalia is similar to that planned for Wellesley. The French reeds are self-explanatory; the Violon in the Great is patterned after similar stops which Bach knew in Thuringia. The eclecticism extends even to the tuning: with five additional "black key" pipes in every octave, three manual divisions and the pedal may be switched from quarter-comma meantone to a Bachian "well-tempered" scheme by moving a lever; the Brustwerk and Brustpedalia are in meantone and the Brustwerk keyboard has two sub-semitones to the octave, as in the Wellesley organ.

Esaias Compenius's magnum opus in Bückeburg... built 1615, destroyed only in 1919, has been a point of departure; influential too has been the work on our new organ for Wellesley College. At the same time, we have included the essentials for playing French classical organ music, namely the Grand Jeux, the Cromorne, and the various jeux de tierce.

Compenius's and Fritzsche's habit of borrowing part of the Pedal from the Great is evident in our design. This suggested itself also because there is really no room for pedal towers in the church gallery.

Harald [Vogel] insisted that the organ be convenient for the organist, and pressed us into devising a good shifting movement for passing back and forth between well temperament and meantone so that we would not have to use split keys. Except for the Brustwerk, which Harald says often possessed the two subsemitones when the other manuals did not, the keyboards of the organ will present a normal appearance to the organist.

If you refer to either the photograph or the drawing, you will see that the Rückpositiv is divided in two cabinets as in Fritzsche's Dresden organ. The Brustpositiv is centered above the organist's head, overhanging somewhat so that it will not deafen him. To the left and right of the Brustpositiv are the two halves of the Brustpedalia. There would be hand-operated cupboard doors for all three Brust openings. The Great, or Werk, would occupy the three large towers and two flats overhead, with 16 foot C of the Prestant in the very center. The two smaller outside towers, and the flats connecting them to the Werk towers, would enclose the Seitenwerk. (We found that the cross bracing for the roof interfered with placing an Oberwerk above the Great; placing the division at the same level as the Great should also make it easier to keep the organ in tune.) The Principal Schweigel 8′ of the Seitenwerk, a somewhat gentle, flutey principal—like the 4 foot in the Wellesley Rückpositiv, would appear in the front.

Charles Fisk to Herbert Nanney, March 8, 1982

During the ensuing year Charles Fisk and Harald Vogel refined the proposed tuning system, and Robert Cornell of the Fisk workshop devised a workable shifting mechanism for it. In response to questions raised by one of Dr. Nanney's students, Fisk offered the following explanation of what was planned:

The basis of what we plan is in *De Organographia* by Michael Praetorius (cf. especially the section on the Dresden court chapel where Schütz held forth). This happens to be what inspired our recent organ at Wellesley College. As I started the research for that organ, I had no idea how much I would pick up in that experiment; it turned out that I had learned a great deal. I had never heard quarter-comma meantone in an organ before Wellesley, and I found there is a very special effect in an organ so tuned because an organ tends to pull itself into tune. Thus, in quarter-comma meantone not only do you have automatically pure octaves and pure major thirds, the fifths and the fourths, if you locate them near each other inside the organ case, will have a tendency to pull themselves into tune. This creates in loud passages a "locked in" sensation, no doubt intended by the composer, that causes the organ to sound more imposing than one would have ever thought possible.

For the Stanford organ my first thought, therefore, was to split the five accidentals so that we would have enough meantone notes to play all of Bach in pure meantone. But we know that Bach hated pure meantone, so we compromised on a fairly acid well-tempered system, with no actual wolf, which can be switched to a fifth-comma meantone. In the circles you can see it is only the five accidentals changing. The fifth-comma meantone works especially well; the major thirds pull into pure thirds (almost) due to natural drawing, and the leading tones are raised enough to keep them from sounding strange.

The organ will have four manuals and pedal. Three of the manuals—and pedal—employ the accidental shifting system; the Brustwerk does not shift but instead is fixed in fifth-comma meantone and has the usual antique short octave: C, D, E, F, F♯, G, G♯, A, A♯, B, C.

Our purpose in building this organ has been to provide a large instrument which can play everything from Praetorius to Bach with all possible authority. We have gone about accomplishing this in a way that has not been tried by anyone before, to the best of my knowledge.

Charles Fisk to Herbert Nanney, March 21, 1983

The Stanford organ was dedicated in a concert by Herbert Nanney on May 6, 1984; additional recitals were given on June 15 by Harald Vogel and on July 1 by Simon Preston. Between these last two the organ was featured in two contrasting recitals during the national convention of the American Guild of Organists—a French classic program by Fenner Douglass and a North German baroque program by Harald Vogel.

I wanted to build an organ that not only will serve as the Memorial Church organ at Stanford, but one that would bring full circle the process that began there for me, a quest for a truly old organ. I wanted old music to spring to life in the way it was written, in a way it hadn't been heard before.

Charles Fisk, interview in *Stanford Observer*, 1982

Although Charles Fisk had drawn up stoplists and/or sketched out plans for three or four subsequent organs, Opus 85 and Opus 84 were the last two organs in which he was directly involved. At the time of his death on December 16, 1983, the Stanford organ was in process of being installed in California, and the Mount Holyoke organ was under construction in the workshop. Despite his illness, he had shaped their tonal and physical designs and overseen all elements of their construction. They, and their predecessors, stand as a testimony to a keen and inquiring mind which was constantly learning, and a restless creative spirit which was ever searching for new ways to express itself.

List of Organs

Andover Organ Company, *Thomas W. Byers and Charles B. Fisk*

OPUS

24 Williamstown, Massachusetts, First Congregational Church
    Rebuild of an electric-action organ, 1956

25 Houston, Texas, Rice University Chapel
    New electric-action organ with slider chests, 1958

26 Newburyport, Massachusetts, First Religious Society (Unitarian)
    Rebuild of an Alley/Hutchings tracker-action organ, 1957

27 Billerica, Massachusetts, First Parish Church (Unitarian)
    Rebuild of a Hamill tracker-action organ, 1957
    (later destroyed by fire)

Andover Organ Company, *Charles B. Fisk, President*

OPUS

28 Lawrence, Massachusetts, Redeemer Lutheran Church
    New tracker-action organ, 1959

29 Contract cancelled

30 Cambridge, Massachusetts, First Congregational Church
    Rebuild of an electric-action unit organ, 1959

31 Westwood, Massachusetts, St. John's Episcopal Church
    New tracker-action organ, Rückpositiv only, 1959

32 Subcontracted to post-1961 Andover Organ Co.

33 Boston, Massachusetts, King's Chapel (Unitarian)
    Addition of mixtures to Skinner organ, 1960

34 South Dennis, Massachusetts, Congregational Church
    Restoration of Snetzler organ, 1959

35 Baltimore, Maryland, Mount Calvary Episcopal Church
    New tracker-action organ, 1961

C. B. Fisk, Inc., *Charles B. Fisk, President*
[N.B. From 1961 on, all organs have tracker action]
OPUS

36   Gloucester, Massachusetts, Independent Christian Church
      Rebuild of Hutchings organ, 1962

37   Wellesley, Massachusetts, Jewett Arts Center, Wellesley College
      New organ, 1962

38   Subcontracted to Andover Organ Co.

39   Subcontracted to Andover Organ Co.

40   Subcontracted to Andover Organ Co.

41   Subcontracted to Andover Organ Co.

42   Cambridge, Massachusetts, Daniel Pinkham residence
      Positiv organ built by Fritz Noack in Fisk shop, 1960

43   Subcontracted to Andover Organ Co.

44   Boston, Massachusetts, King's Chapel (Unitarian)
      New organ, 1964

45   Westerly, Rhode Island, Christ Episcopal Church
      New organ, 1965

46   Cambridge, Massachusetts, Memorial Church, Harvard University
      New organ, 1967

47   Boston, Massachusetts, Boston University School of Fine Arts
      New organ, 1965

48   Greencastle, Indiana, St. Paul's Roman Catholic Church
      New organ, 1965

48A Greencastle, Indiana, DePauw University
      New organ, 1965

49   Belmont, Massachusetts, First Church of Christ, Scientist
      New organ, 1968

50   Winchester, Massachusetts, First Congregational Church
      New organ, 1969

LIST OF ORGANS

51 Souderton, Pennsylvania, Zion Mennonite Church
    New organ, 1969

52 Greencastle, Indiana, St. Paul's Roman Catholic Church
    New organ, 1968
    (moved to St. Meinrad's Seminary, St. Meinrad, Indiana)

53 Boston, Massachusetts, St. Stephen's Roman Catholic Church
    Rebuild of early Boston-built organ, 1967

54 New Haven, Connecticut, First Church of Christ (Center Church)
    New organ, 1971; Brustwerk completed 1974

55 Boston, Massachusetts, Old West Church (United Methodist)
    New organ, 1971

56 Collinsville, Connecticut, Trinity Episcopal Church
    New organ, 1971

57 Willimantic, Connecticut, St. Paul's Episcopal Church
    New organ, 1972

58 Contract cancelled

59 Winston-Salem, North Carolina, North Carolina School of the Arts
    New organ, 1969

59A Newton, Massachusetts, Frank Taylor residence
    New organ, 1969
    (moved to St. Barnabas' Episcopal Church, Falmouth, Massachusetts)

60 Contract cancelled

61 Lowell, Massachusetts, First United Baptist Church
    Rebuild of a Hook organ, 1972

62 Ipswich, Massachusetts, Ascension Memorial Episcopal Church
    New organ, 1974

63 Contract cancelled

64 Minneapolis, Minnesota, University of Minnesota, Music School
    New positive organ, 1974

65 Winchester, Massachusetts, Parish of the Epiphany (Episcopal)
    New organ, 1974

- 66A Boston, Massachusetts, New England Conservatory
  New positive organ, 1974

- 66B New Haven, Connecticut, Yale University School of Music
  New positive organ, 1974

- 67 Huntington, Indiana, Central Christian Church
  New organ, 1976

- 68 Burlington, Vermont, University of Vermont, School of Music
  New organ, 1976

- 69 Marblehead, Massachusetts, St. Michael's Episcopal Church
  New organ, 1975

- 70 Cazenovia, New York, First Presbyterian Church
  New organ, 1976

- 71 Westfield, Massachusetts, First Congregational Church
  New organ, 1977

- 72 Wellesley, Massachusetts, Houghton Chapel, Wellesley College
  New organ, 1981

- 73 Subcontracted to A. David Moore & Co.

- 74 Providence, Rhode Island, St. Peter's & St. Andrew's Church
  New organ, 1977

- 75 Winston-Salem, North Carolina, North Carolina School of the Arts
  New organ, 1977

- 76 Durham, North Carolina, Duke University School of Music
  New organ, 1978

- 76A Princeton, New Jersey, Westminster Choir College
  New organ, 1978

- 77 Durham, North Carolina, Duke University School of Music
  New organ, 1978

- 77A Atlanta, Georgia, St. Bartholomew's Episcopal Church
  New organ, 1978

- 78 St. Paul, Minnesota, House of Hope Presbyterian Church
  New organ, 1979

LIST OF ORGANS

- 79   Charleston, West Virginia, First Presbyterian Church
  New organ, 1980
- 80   Contract cancelled
- 81   Storrs, Connecticut, Storrs Congregational Church
  New organ, 1981
- 82   Greensboro, North Carolina, Christ United Methodist Church
  New organ, 1982
- 83   Rochester, New York, Downtown United Presbyterian Church
  New organ, 1983
- 84   South Hadley, Massachusetts, Abbey Chapel, Mount Holyoke College
  New organ, 1984
- 85   Stanford, California, Memorial Church, Stanford University
  New organ, 1984

[The following organs were built by C. B. Fisk, Inc. after the death of Charles Fisk, or remain to be built.]

- 86   Pacific Palisades, California, St. Matthew's Parish, 1985
- 87   Ann Arbor, Michigan, University of Michigan, 1985
- 88   Woodberry Forest, Virginia, Woodberry Forest School, 1985
- 89   New Bern, North Carolina, First Presbyterian Church, 1986
- 90   Las Cruces, New Mexico, University of New Mexico
- 91   Portola Valley, California, Jacques Littlefield residence
- 92   New York, New York, Church of the Transfiguration
- 93   Niantic, Connecticut, St. John's Episcopal Church
- 94   Dayton, Ohio, St. George's Episcopal Church
- 95   Buffalo, New York, State University of New York
- 96   (reserved)
- 97   Gloucester, Massachusetts, St. John's Episcopal Church

98   Evansville, Indiana, First Presbyterian Church
99   Houston, Texas, Palmer Memorial Episcopal Church
100 (reserved)
101 Dallas, Texas, Southern Methodist University

Photographs, Sketches, and Diagrams

Opus 35, 1961. Baltimore, Maryland. Mount Calvary Episcopal Church.
CREDIT: Smithsonian Institution.

Opus 44, 1964. Boston, Massachusetts. King's Chapel.
CREDIT: Robert Cornell.

Opus 45, 1965. Westerly, Rhode Island. Christ Episcopal Church.
CREDIT: Robert Cornell.

Opus 46, 1967. Cambridge, Massachusetts. Memorial Church, Harvard University.
CREDIT: Robert Cornell.

Opus 54, 1971. New Haven, Connecticut. First Church of Christ (Center Church).
CREDIT: Barbara Owen.

Opus 55, 1971. Boston, Massachusetts. Old West Church.
CREDIT: Robert Cornell.

Opus 57, 1972. Willimantic, Connecticut. St. Paul's Episcopal Church.
CREDIT: Robert Cornell.

Opus 66B, 1974. New Haven, Connecticut. Yale University School of Music.
CREDIT: Courtesy of C.B. Fisk, Inc.

Opus 71, 1977. Westfield, Massachusetts. First Congregational Church.
CREDIT: Robert Cornell.

Opus 72, 1981. Wellesley, Massachusetts. Houghton Chapel, Wellesley College.
CREDIT: Robert Cornell.

Opus 76A, 1978. Princeton, New Jersey. Westminster Choir College.
CREDIT: Barbara Owen.

Opus 78, 1979. St. Paul, Minnesota. House of Hope Presbyterian Church.
CREDIT: Robert Cornell.

Opus 79, 1980. Charleston, West Virginia. First Presbyterian Church.
CREDIT: Robert Cornell.

Opus 83, 1983. Rochester, New York. Downtown United Presbyterian Church.
CREDIT: Robert Cornell.

Opus 84, 1984. South Hadley, Massachusetts. Abbey Chapel, Mount Holyoke College.
CREDIT: Michael Brown.

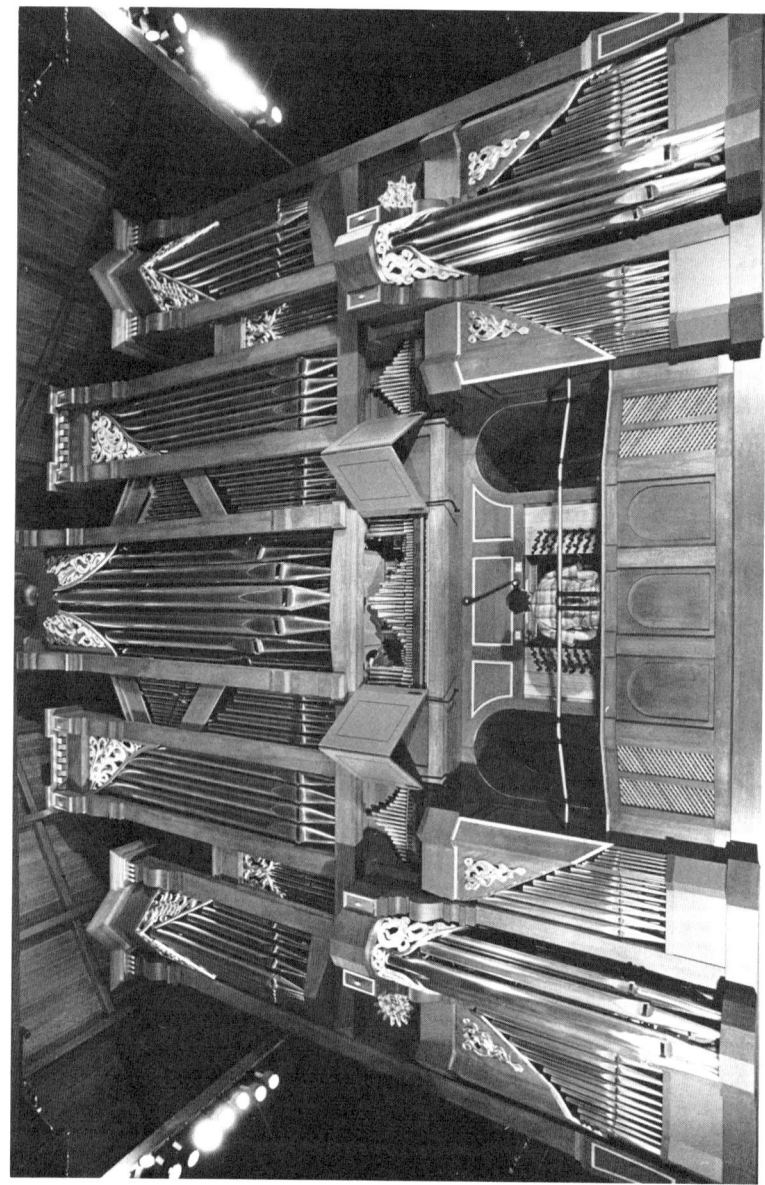

Opus 85, 1984. Stanford, California. Memorial Church, Stanford University.
CREDIT: Chuck Painter.

PHOTOGRAPHS, SKETCHES, AND DIAGRAMS 99

Charles Fisk and Donald Willing.
CREDIT: Lenscraft Photos, Inc. Courtesy of Yuko Hayashi.

Charles Fisk and Frank Taylor examining Dom Bedos.
CREDIT: Robert Cornell.

Charles Fisk voicing the Wellesley organ.
CREDIT: Paul Foley.

Charles Fisk at the voicing jack of the Fisk shop.
CREDIT: Julie O'Neil.

PHOTOGRAPHS, SKETCHES, AND DIAGRAMS 103

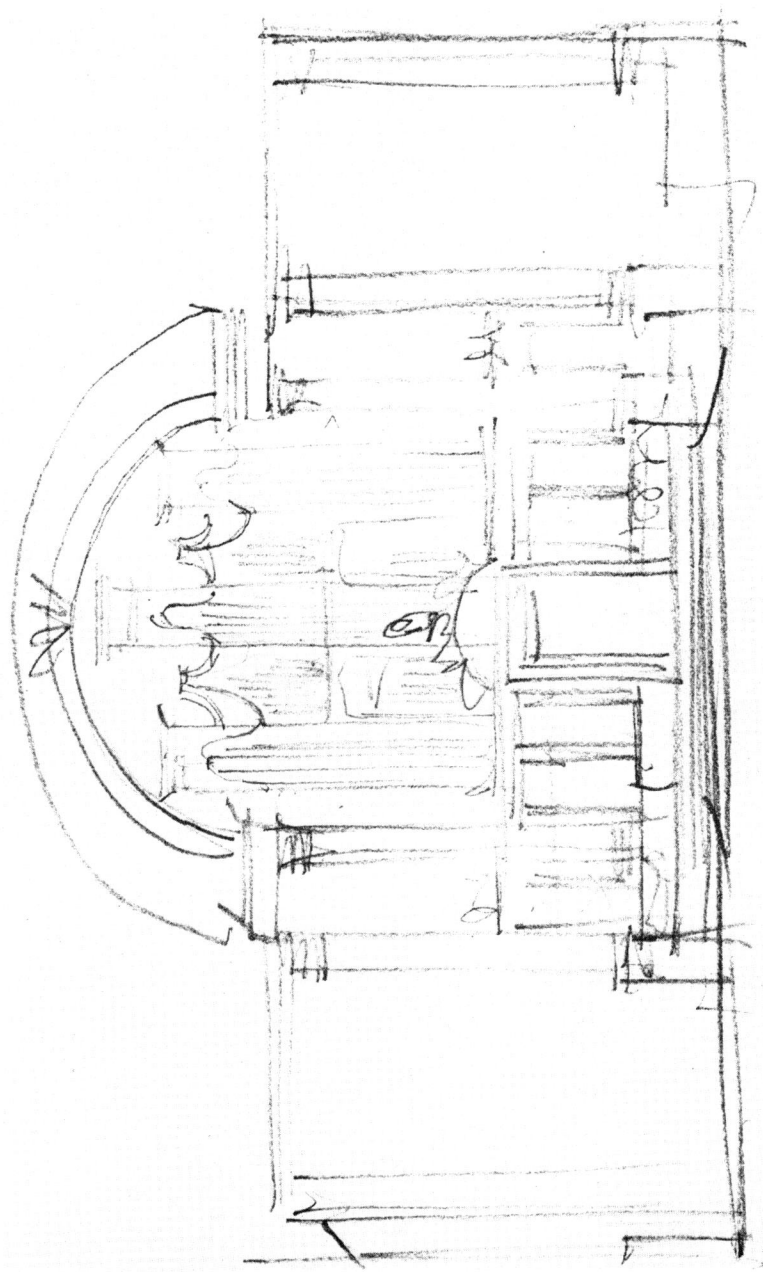

Sketch for the organ in Memorial Church (Appleton Chapel), Harvard University.
CREDIT: Charles Fisk. Dated March of 1963.

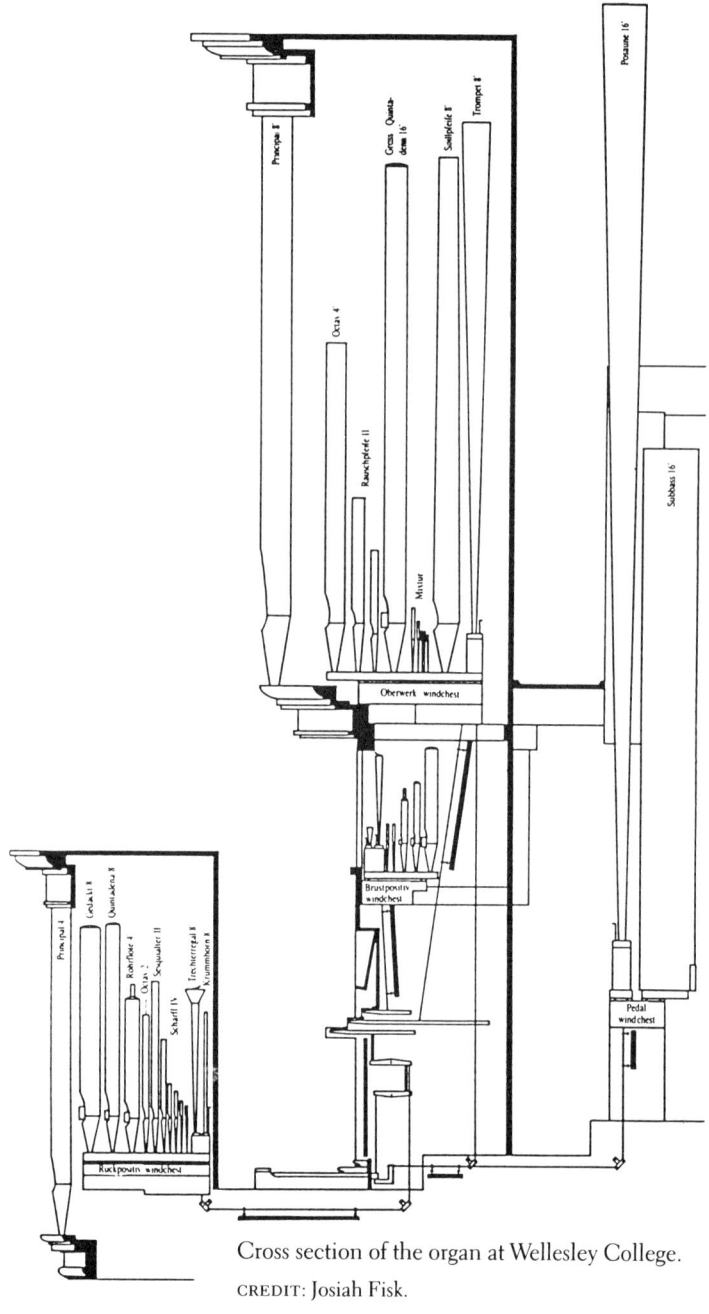

Cross section of the organ at Wellesley College.
CREDIT: Josiah Fisk.

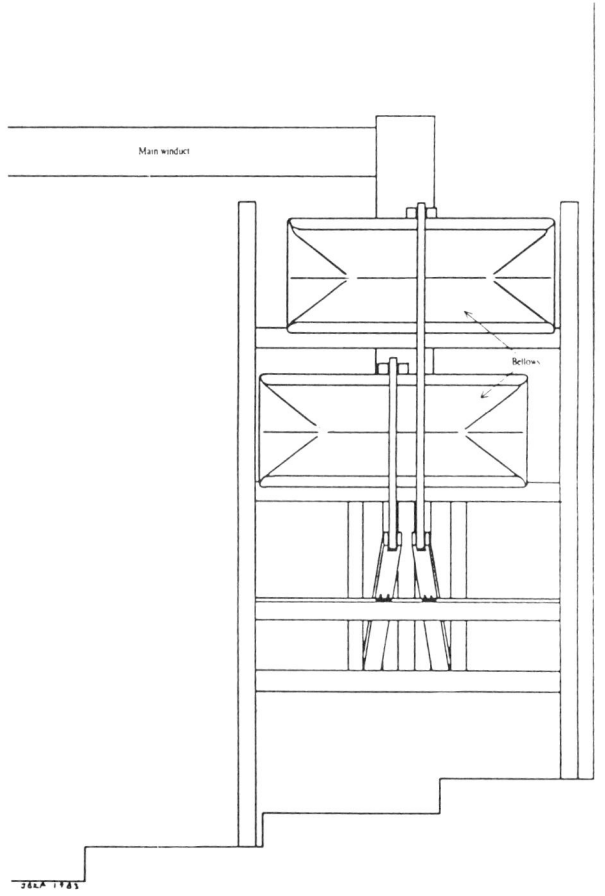

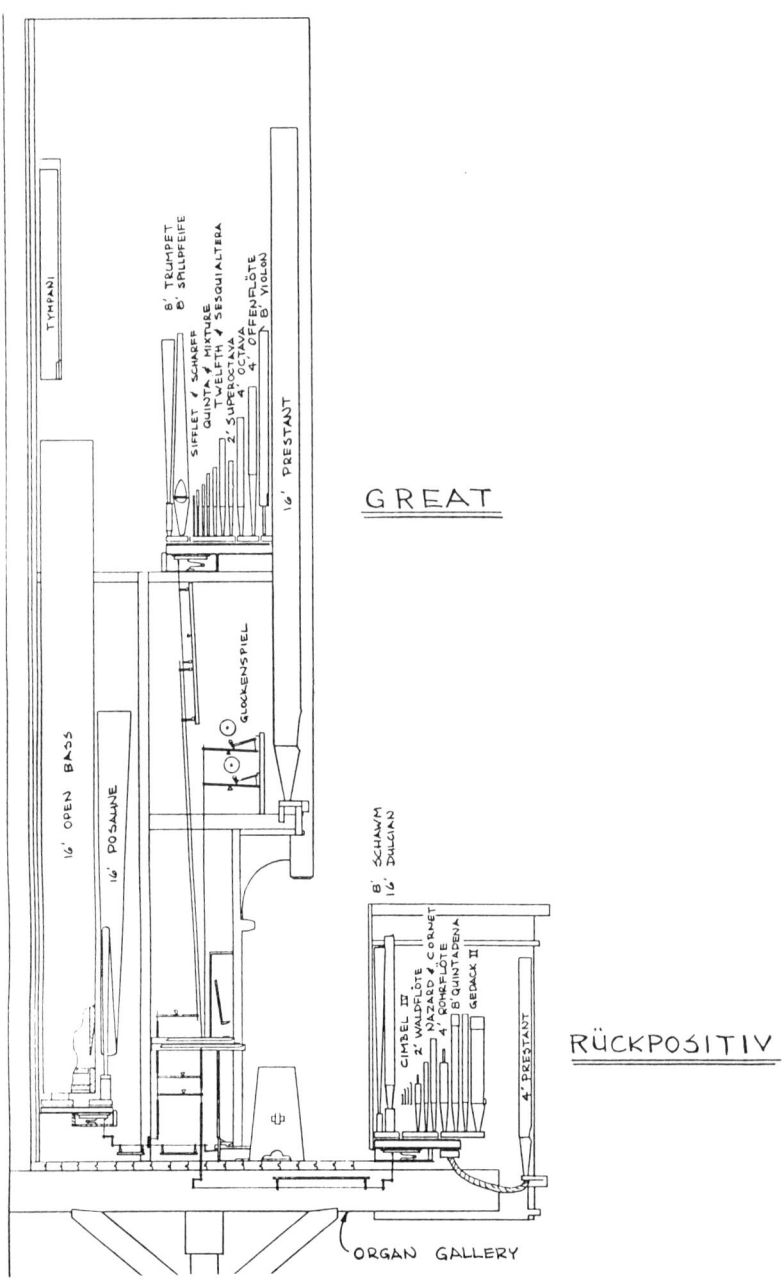

Cross section of the organ at Mount Holyoke College.
CREDIT: Robert Cornell.

PHOTOGRAPHS, SKETCHES, AND DIAGRAMS

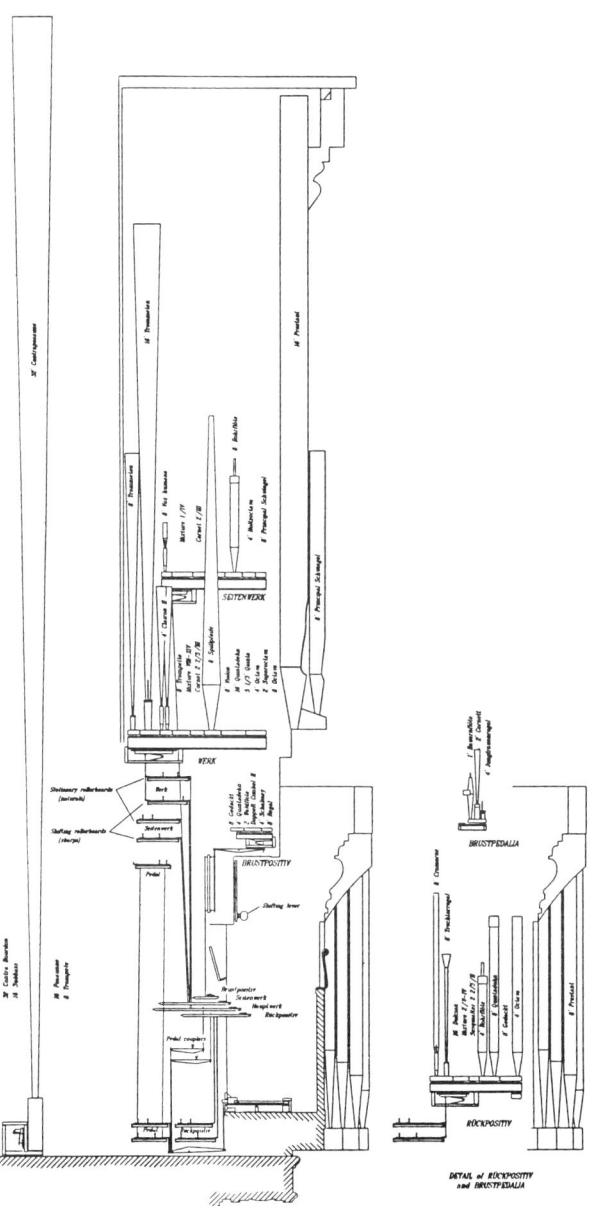

Cross section of the organ at Stanford University.
CREDIT: Robert Cornell.

WRITINGS OF CHARLES FISK

PUBLISHED ARTICLES

The Architect as Organ Maker

AXIOM: PLACEMENT is the most important of the factors which determine the effectiveness of an organ. That is to say, the way in which the pipes of an organ are arranged among themselves and then situated within a building has largely to do with the way the organ will ultimately sound. Or as a physicist might say, "In both designing an organ and placing it in a building, the *geometry* must be given greater weight than any other factor."

It is not possible to prove the truth of this axiom here; indeed the truth of it emerges only out of long and often bitter experience in which one has attempted to disregard it. Ask an organophile what makes a good organ and he will probably mention choice of stops, scaling and voicing of the pipes, acoustical reverberation period of the building, etc. etc. Or perhaps he will even mention placement (or geometry if he is a physicist), but he is not likely to put it at the top of the list as I have. Despite that, let us begin here by *assuming* that our Placement Axiom is in fact axiomatic, and then let us see what conditional conclusions can be deduced from it.

CONCLUSION I. The architect of the building has *primary control* over the organ builder's chances for providing a fine instrument. He sets an upper limit to the quality of the organ, as it were, for he provides the building and the site for the organ in the first place. Now it is common to hear church musicians inveigh against the architect of such and such a building for making it "dead" acoustically, perhaps by permitting wall to wall carpet or by using acoustic (actually *an*acoustic) plaster or tile, so that reverberation time is cut to minimum. Indeed, this *is* a grievous crime, which architects and church committees too often commit against music's estate; yet by our Placement Axiom it is not as grievous as sinking the organ pipes in that lateral abyss known as the organ chamber (much as if they were part of the plumbing or heating), or putting them on random display out in the open.

CONCLUSION II. From Conclusion I and the Placement Axiom, it follows that organs will be good only if architects make a serious attempt to understand what an organ really is and how it works. In a sense, *architects are actually organ builders*, and I hope they will not cringe when I say that they have been making a rather bad job of their organ building in the past century or so. I do not really mean to pretend here that the parlous state in which the church organ presently finds itself can be laid at the church architect's door—he after all has only provided in the long run what ministers, congregations, organists and organ builders have thought pleasing—but architects, by their disregard of what organs might be, i.e., by lack of imagination vis-a-vis the organ, have certainly helped the instrument's downfall. To put it more constructively, were architects suddenly to take an intelligent interest in the organ, there would unquestionably be a striking change in the usefulness and the quality of the instrument. The current rise of the electronic organ-substitute is partly the work of architects who in the first place helped the organ to take on the nature of musical air-conditioning equipment, and who, now that the chambers required for such equipment are so expensive, have turned to the electronic "organ" for space saving reasons.

CONCLUSION III. If architects are indeed organ builders, it then follows that they have always been organ builders, and that they are in part responsible for the way in which the organ has evolved. In other words, they are in part responsible for its original glory as well as its recent downfall. This statement requires an historical explanation:

The organ, to the Romans a secular instrument, found haven in the medieval monasteries and emerged from the middle ages as *the* church instrument. Why? I think it was primarily because of the type of building which medieval church architects provided. These were lofty buildings made largely of stone; acoustically they were very live—long reverberation time—which meant that any sound made within was sustained for several seconds by the building. (Hence the concept of the building itself as a musical instrument.) Percussive sounds, or sounds of short duration, fare poorly in such buildings. Sustained tones, however, such as the notes of an organ, are received sympathetically; the initial note is simply added to by the sustaining property of the building, and the effect after holding the note for two or three seconds is as if the tone were emanating from every corner of the room, which indeed it is. This effect, known in acoustics as diffusion, in which the listener is surrounded by his sound sources, is extremely pleasing to the ear and is aesthetically apposite to the visual effect of these lofty buildings.

Since a reverberant building reinforces a weak sustained note in such a way as to make it seem pervasive, and since it reinforces only the harmonic content of a coarse sound, the early organs, whether feeble or coarse or both, produced a singularly happy result in the environment provided by the medieval church architect. Within this environment, during the three centuries from 1400 to 1700, organ culture grew in complexity and elegance until, by the early part of the 18th century, a pinnacle was reached. If we cannot exactly relate the decline of the instrument in the last two hundred years to the decline of reverberation-time in church buildings—it is more correct to relate both to other historical parameters—we can certainly remark that organs do sound uninspiring in dead churches, and goodness knows we have an adequacy of these at present.

I have just said that the organ grew up in live buildings and I have implied that in consequence a live building is almost essential to the tonal health of the organ enclosed within it. All true, but what has this to do with our Placement Axiom? To explain, I must continue our history:

The earliest and simplest music widely used in the medieval church building was plain chant, a purely melodic form of vocal music. Plain chant too could not have developed without the live building, for it is the overlaying of each new tone upon the reverberating "tail" of the tones just previously sung that makes plain chant effective. For pure melody, placement of the musicians would not have been critical; however, as soon as more complicated music of two separate contrapuntal parts was essayed, musicians must have realized that the *linear*, or *horizontal*, ideas they wished to express ended up in confusion unless they chose carefully the vantage point for their singing. Thus arose recognition of the importance of source-placement in the live building, for complex music requires that the listener be able to understand its "consonants" (transients) as well as its "vowels," whether produced by voices or by musical instruments.

The simplest rule to remember is this: If a building is live, and if you really want the listener to hear the consonants in music, or in speech for that matter, it is necessary to provide him with strong direct sound from the source so as to overcome the "vowel predominance" of the reverberating building. This implies first that you establish the entire source of sound in the building so that it is plainly *visible* to the listener ("line-of-sight transmission") since sound, like light, travels a straight path. Second, you can reinforce the direct sound by placing behind the source a close-fitting reflecting shell, like a band shell—indeed, the classical organ case was a kind of wooden band shell. Sound which the source emits toward the shell is bounced back toward the listener almost immediately; thus, if the explosive consonant "t" is uttered, the "t" which the listener hears coming directly from the source is followed almost immediately by the "t" reflected off the shell, and for the listener the two sounds coalesce into a single consonant, the one sound reinforcing the other. Of course, if the shell is placed a large distance behind the source, then the reflected "t" is late in reaching the listener and he hears the two "t's" separately, the reflection then being heard as an *echo* of the direct sound, and therefore a hindrance to the listener's understanding.

A third measure taken for the sake of the consonants in music—and this is of particular concern to architects—is to place the source of sound where the walls and ceiling of the room, like the close fitting shell just mentioned, will give off *early* reflections which coalesce with the direct sound. The medieval organ was almost always placed with its back against a wall, which in addition to the wooden shell (case) provided early reflections for the intensification of the direct sound. A favorite site for the organ came to be the west gallery; this usually placed the organ as close as possible to both the ceiling and the walls of the tunnel-like clerestory, all of which gave off early reflections of each consonant emitted by the organ. In a long, reverberant building with a lofty west gallery organ it is sometimes astonishing to note the clarity with which the organ speaks, even when conversation between individuals randomly situated at floor level is impossible due to liveness. Clearly, the medieval architects who gave us vaulting clerestories and galleries in stone also gave us, indirectly, plain chant and the motet, sung mass and the chorale, the prelude and fugue, for so much is the virtue of good architecture that it can be the cultural making of the people it serves. These timeless works of musical art, in their proper architectural setting, with strict attention to the rules for good source placement, are breathtakingly beautiful even to our well-assaulted ears, and inspire many to attempt to recapture their sound for use in our modern churches. For a hundred reasons, many of them good, our churches differ greatly from the medieval, whence arises the question, how best to compromise and still retain some vestige of the original tonal effect? Heretofore, as I have implied, emphasis has been concentrated on the long reverberation time of the medieval church. The heart of many a musician has broken when, often simply for lack of height, new buildings have turned up with less than two seconds' reverberation, today regarded as the absolute minimum for church music, though meager compared to the four-to-eight seconds of the medieval church. Yet it is my experience that the medieval musician's solution to his own clarity problem in the live environment, namely good placement, can be of great help in the dead environment. Thus we have a final conclusion:

CONCLUSION IV. By the Placement Axiom, we can have hope for *reasonable* success of a good organ in an acoustically undistinguished building, since there is nearly always the possibility of placing the organ well; indeed, poor placement results only when the building is conceived without paying any real attention to the needs of organ and choir.

The Organ's Breath of Life

THE ORGAN IS NOTHING BUT A MACHINE, whose machine-made sounds will always be without interest unless they can appear to be coming from a living organism. The organ has to *seem* to be alive.

A motorcar is the same. Bucket of bolts we may call it, but the very epithet reflects simultaneously our affection for it and our wonder that a thing made out of bolts et cetera can seem to be so truly alive. And its makers, knowing well what they are about, give it two eyes, a nose and a mouth, sleekness, a look as if crouching ready to spring, the pretty name of a creature. For they know that if the car is to be loved, it must be loved as though it were a living thing.

Some people think of the human body as a machine. Never does it seem more so than when the life has gone out of it and we are left asking, What is this life-catalyst that takes the nuts and bolts of this world and binds them into so mysteriously marvelous, so transcendent a being?

For the organ, the ultimate source of life is of course the player. We organ builders have trouble remembering this. We would gladly build if we could a machine which would do all that is musically possible without the player. Yet past efforts to bypass the player have resulted in works of only temporary attractiveness, and underneath we know our job is to make instruments which faithfully transmit the player's aliveness—when he is alive—and (unfortunately) his deadness when his playing is dead. Whence comes the remark, "A good organ will sound both better and worse than a poor one."

Granted that the player's role is transcendent, what are the ways in which we organ builders can enhance the as-if-alive quality in our instruments? For well over a decade our journals have belabored the pros and cons of ideas which contribute to it. All the talk about the responsive touch of tracker action and the lively effect of unnicked pipes on slider chests is germane here. Yet the talk, centering always around specifics, has not told us everything, and meanwhile all of us tire of hearing about the specifics, particularly when adherence thereto does not necessarily bring about the construction of an artistic instrument. There must then be other specifics than the now-familiar ones, and beyond them must be a generality, a single principle which generates them.

A prime characteristic of the life force on earth is what Wallace Stevens calls the *passion for order*. In organ construction it seems that those terms which promote order, organization, integration—those which pull the instrument together—are the terms which foster the as-if-alive quality. The note channel of the slider chest tending to synchronize the frequencies of the pipes standing above it; the tracker action tending to bind the player physically to his instrument; the chiff of lightly-nicked pipes tending by their unanimity of speech over the same note channel to express the solidarity of the "werk"; these are all well-known examples of integrating forces. And all are part of this life-oriented passion for order, which does indeed seem to be the single principle underlying any good musical instrument.

What are some of the less understood specific forces for order that are rightfully a part of an organ? Let us now discuss the least understood of these, namely, the wind.

As everyone knows, the standard test for the wind system of an organ is to draw all the stops, hold a note in the treble, and repeat a thick chord in the bass. If the treble note gives out not a tortured sound, but remains serene as the Star of Bethlehem, the organ is said to have a "perfect" wind supply. Yet, when we apply this test to the best instruments of ages other than our own, we find scarcely one that passes it. In virtually all of these instruments the wind is unsteady by our standards. Of course, the matter may be dismissed by observing that only in the twentieth century has it become possible to obtain steady wind, and the ancients would no doubt have provided steady wind if they had known how. But by now we should know enough to give this kind of argument its skeptical due; works of art founded on inadequacies always turn inadequacy to their own account: The inadequacies simply become essentials. And so it often is with the unsteady wind of old organs.

Consider as an example the organ at Steinkirchen in Germany, a two-manual organ by Schnitger, with much pipework from even earlier builders. This instrument is a national monument, has a pedigree, is a good example of what Schnitger was all about. It has slider chests, tracker action, individual cabinets for each division, nickless flues, open toes, imitation carved casework—all the officially prescribed nutrients of a healthy North German antique. It is in a farmer's church, and its sound has the endearingly naturalistic, homespun, homely, barnyard quality it ought therefore to have. And what contributes more than anything else to this quality? The wind supply. If you attempt to apply the standard test for steady wind to it, the organ sounds as if it would positively tip over. Steinkirchen has the most elastic, loose-connected sounding wind system imaginable, and the entire effect of the organ is colored by it. Indeed, this writer presumes that if the wind supply at Steinkirchen were to be replaced by a system of the modern *Schwimmer* type, or the Universal Air Chest type, the organ's very special quality would vanish.

Steinkirchen is folk art; therefore many of its features cause us to smile. The unsteady wind surely seems to be a joke—and yet it is the kind of joke which, at the right moment, can bring tears to the eyes. Another time it can be a rude joke, out of place—ugly, even. The very variableness of the effect of the wind upon music of diverse kinds suggests the instrument has a temper, that it likes one player but not another, one composer but not another. It seems alive. You even seem to hear it breathing.

What characterizes the wind of organs like *Steinkirchen*, and what is the physical origin of the sounds created? Such organs were always hand-blown. Two or more bellows—diagonal bellows like fireplace bellows, only much larger, perhaps one yard by two yards—were situated by the builder in some convenient place well behind the organ, often in the church tower. These were set horizontally, each bellows with its lower leaf fixed. Each upper leaf, free to rise and fall, was loaded with enough stone to yield the organ's wind pressure, say, 2½ inches. The organ blower's job was to go from one bellows to the other lifting the upper leaves one by one (bellows inhaling) and gently letting them rest "on the wind" (bellows exhaling). As long as at least one bellows was exhaling, that was enough to keep the organ playing. Whenever the organ blower saw that his last bellows was about exhausted, he would raise the upper leaf of a neighboring bellows to be sure the organ would not run out of wind. Note that these bellows *combined* the functions of feeder and reservoir.

From the bellows stack a single wooden duct of modest rectangular cross section (say, 4 inches by 10 inches) traversed the distance to the organ case. There the duct divided into ducts of somewhat smaller section and these led to the windboxes of the several windchests in the organ. It is significant that these windboxes were seldom much larger in cross section than the ducts which fed them.

Under such an arrangement, when the organist plays a key and the corresponding chest valve opens, the windbox and duct, being small, cannot provide out of their own "compression capacity" the necessary first flush of air. Therefore the chest pressure must drop momentarily, and chest pressure is not restored to normal until the long air column leading back to the bellows is set in motion. The result of opening the valve is thus a single downward pulse in the chest pressure, lasting a fraction of a second. (In the best wind systems the single pulse is all that occurs; there are no attendant repercussions of pressure, such as may occur in systems where the cross section of the windbox is much larger than that of the duct which feeds the windbox.) In corollary fashion, if the pallet valve has been open for some time and is then shut, the exact reverse occurs; there is a single upward pulse in the chest wind pressure due to the overage of wind sliding along the long duct and crowding into the wind chest after no more wind is needed. Often this positive pulse on closing is more audible than the negative pulse on opening.

One's first thought is that these two kinds of pulse, negative and positive, would be detrimental to the making of music. For most of the old music, quite the opposite is true. For example, consider how the pulses contribute to clarity in counterpoint: Assume a five-voice fugue of the classical sort being played on *organo pleno*. Ordinarily it is easy to hear motion in the soprano and bass lines because they are "on the outside." But what of motion in the tenor line while the other four voices are sounding, but momentarily fixed—how will this motion ever be heard? At Steinkirchen, each time you move the tenor voice—each time one pallet is shut to end one note and another is opened to begin the next—there is in the wind a positive pulse followed immediately by a negative pulse, both of which will be manifest as fluctuations in the sustained tones of the other four voices. In this way the sustained voices help to *mark* the comings and goings of an inner part, instead of simply masking it.

Quite certainly this effect has had to do with the very origins of organ counterpoint in late medieval Europe. After all, why sustain parts at all, when what you wish to hear is the motion of an inner part? And why write music for several voices in which, for example, there is without fail a change in at least one voice on every eighth note of the piece? We hear motion in the soprano and bass lines because they are "on the outside." But what of the inner voices? We have always known music of this sort was something of a game whose object it was to see which voice would change next, and how? But is it not also a game to see what the organ wind will tell us, through the non-moving, sustained notes?

The whole subject of the wind is fascinating and elusive, and this writer makes no pretense at a thorough understanding of it. He can, however, put forth questions which, either in this country or abroad, might provoke further thought:

1. Classically, isn't a fine legato touch simply the art of closing one pallet just at the exact moment of opening the next, in order that the positive and negative pulses in the wind shall cancel out, leaving the wind undisturbed?
2. Is it possible that the apparently drab fantasies and voluntaries, particularly those out of sixteenth and seventeenth century England, are primarily essays in the handling of organ wind? When to disturb the wind deliberately, and when not? These pieces always come to life on the instruments of their time, instruments whose small-bore wind systems labor over the stable production of so much as three voices of counterpoint.
3. Is the lack of chiff in early English organs (and consequently in the earliest American organs) due to the fact that the wind pulses are actually a substitute for chiff? The whole art of English chamber organ building seems to center around artfully starving an organ of its wind.
4. What role did unsteady wind play in the evolution of ornamentation in European music? After all, in many old organs, every time a pallet opens to make a pipe sound, the attendant negative pulse causes the pipe to swoop up to its note slightly, after the manner of an upward appogiatura (♪○). In the Rückpositivs of some old organs where the wind ducts are particularly under-

sized, the wind supply gives actually a little *port de voix* at the beginning of each note (♪𝄿). Did these "obligatory ornaments" suggest the use of ornaments generally? Or were the multitudinous ornaments in the early French and English music put there to cover up these repercussions in the wind, or perhaps to give the organist control over them, i.e., to make them the organist's thing instead of the organ's thing?

5. If we accept that, for the organ, wind is one of the unifying forces mentioned previously, isn't it then probable that all divisions of an organ should draw their wind from the same bellows? This means that the pulses from one keyboard will be marked in the sustained notes of another; it also means that the sounds of full organ, coming as it were from one giant pair of lungs, will have a unity of mass achievable in no other way. The ancients pursued this policy except in their large instruments.

6. What about the tuning of organs? Our current concern over fine tuning presumes a very steady wind supply originating with an electric blower. But with the ancients there was the bellows boy whose every bored indiscretion no doubt shook the wind to the tuner's distraction, and there was the variation in pressure due to the fact that a bellow's pressure increases between the nearly open position and the nearly closed. Clearly, tuning at that time was not as good as we should like it. Yet there is reason to believe that detuned pipes are not as much of an annoyance in an old organ as in a new one. Recall that in a modern organ the bothersome thing about a mixture note out of tune is, every time the note returns in the music you are subjected to exactly the same burble, and after a while it "gets to you"; you become sensitized to that one note. Now suppose that instead of being rock-steady, the wind supply is full of all sorts of ripple, partly due to the pulses of valves opening and closing, and partly due to manual organ blowing. This ripple causes, in all notes of the mixture, burbles which appear to combine with the burbles of detuning, but because they add a random component, the mind does not become sensitized—the mind can *see through* the "defect" and is therefore free to concentrate on the music. To be sure, the defect will remain noticeable, and may cause us to smile, but it will not become an obsession.

Like all of the integrating terms which are part of the passion for order, the introduction of the right sort of unsteady wind into an organ increases the problems for the organist. Just as the fidelity of tracker action makes it essential that the player get his notes rhythmical and right, so the unsteady wind creates a problem for the player which can be likened to the problem of small-boat-handling. The feeling of commencing a piece on unsteady wind is somehow like stepping from a low, solid dock onto the floorboard of a rather tippy dory—one does it with care, one feels the water give under his weight, one realizes that if he steps too near the edge he may capsize. A serene legato is like rowing this dory flawlessly across the harbor, so that all you can hear is the click of the oar locks. Rougher music is like rough water: She labors in the troughs but is buoyed up on the crests. (The sense of buoyancy is very strong in the old organs.) Notice that one says "*She* labors . . . "—a sure sign that a boat is an as-if-alive thing, and that it has been so regarded for centuries. Indeed, if one thinks about it, one realizes that organs and sea-going craft have a great deal in common.

The writer would not have the reader imagine that a complete return to the winding principles of Steinkirchen is really practical. No organ builder today would dare to build an organ exactly like Steinkirchen unless he had a specific order to do so. One cannot build a service instrument which shakes like a willow on a Mendelssohn anthem accompaniment, however buoyant its Buxtehude may be. But it *is* possible to make wind systems which are a flexible compromise. Too many hard-sounding wind supplies are being built today, especially in Europe. Modern European organ building practice has taught us much, and still has many things to teach us, but this writer does not believe the winding of an organ is one of them. We need to apply our own minds and our own ears to the task of discovering what makes organ music come alive under the player's fingers.

Finally, the writer wishes it understood that only a certain kind of instability is desirable in a wind supply. Most of the instability encountered, especially in organs built in the twentieth century, is gross to say the least and is, in fact, what has given wind flexibility a bad name.

[Editor's note: "The Organ's Breath of Life" is perhaps the best known of Charles Fisk's writings, not the least because of the controversy which briefly followed it in the Letters-to-the-Editor column and elsewhere. There were the usual accusations of "antiquarianism," some misunderstandings, and some agreement. In a letter dated October 22, 1971, to Mark Stansbury, who had written to express his agreement with Fisk's views, Fisk elaborated on and clarified some of his statements:]

> I was pleased to receive your letter of September 11. To date it represents about one third of the total fan mail I received as a result of my article in *The Diapason*. Indeed, the primary result of the article has been to cost us a couple of contracts, our prospective clients suddenly having noticed that the organs we have been building all these years had slightly unsteady wind, which to these people didn't seem right. Prior to the article the instability had passed unnoticed.
>
> Nevertheless I am absolutely certain that my thesis is correct and that it will one day become canon.
>
> You are quite right that Clutton's "lipping effect" at Steinkirchen is largely due to the wind characteristic. Just after the valve first opens, there is a deficit of wind. As air moves down the wind trunk to eliminate the

deficit, the pitch of the pipe rises, causing what could be called a lipping effect. This whole affair is the negative pulse of which I speak in the article.

You are also right in assuming that a greater length of wind duct produces more flexibility. This is a complex problem indeed, but if one regards the bellows or reservoir as a source of steady pressure, then the elasticity of the air in a long duct, leading away from a stable source, invites pressure fluctuations at the remote end. Actually, of course, the fluctuations produced at the remote end then travel the length of the duct and disturb the stability of the bellows itself, so that bellows and duct are actually a single vibrating system.

My impression is that if the duct in question is fairly large in cross section (say one foot square) and quite long (say, thirty feet) the natural frequency of the system becomes so low that it no longer disturbs the listener. I have never had opportunity to verify this by experiment.

To achieve the results of antiquity it seems essential to keep the pallet box of the wind chest small in cross section; in other words, the pallet box should not be significantly greater in cross section than the duct which feeds it. This rule is continually breached by modern organ builders, and makes for an unpleasant unsteadiness, particularly in pitman chest organs.

In my opinion the worst habit of the modern organ builder is the (growing) use of the schwimmer, the quick-responding regulator built into the bottom of the wind chest. This device precludes any unsteadiness of wind except for vibrations in the range of the vibrations produced by the pipes themselves, which the ear tends to attribute to the speech of pipes rather than to fluctuations in wind pressure. Not only does the schwimmer thus give the illusion of steadiness while upsetting the speech characteristic of the pipes; it also denies the possibility of pleasant fluctuations of the wind supply. Although I hardly mentioned it, the schwimmer was what I was really writing against in my article.

Unless I receive a whole lot more mail like the letter you sent me, I shall not be writing any more articles for the journals. On the other hand, a useful purpose would be served if persons such as yourself would write *The Diapason* raising the wind issue again. It is far from a dead subject. The more people train themselves to listen for this aspect of tone production in the organ, the more they will come to recognize it as an essential part of the old music.

"The organ is a machine. Organ builder's object is to keep it from seeming so.
   1. Make it responsive to human touch, so that the human's qualities will become markworthy over and above the machine.

2. Try to bring mystery into the voicing of the pipes. If pipes have no mystery, or are defective, the defects sensitize the ear to themselves so that the defects are inescapable and ruin the music.
3. Give the wind an animated quality, like a creature.
   a. Let whole organ speak on one source of air."

[Charles Fisk, notes jotted on a worksheet, March 1969]

Pipe Flueways

Here in these pages I would like to stir discussion of a voicing question that has troubled American organ building for 25 years. *How narrow should we be making our flues?* (Remember, the flue, or windway, is the little slit that takes the air from the pipe foot and forms it into the wind sheet, which in turn undulates across the upper lip, causing the air column in the pipe to vibrate. The flue is where the nicking goes.)

American flue history reads like this: From Hook and Erben in the 19th century to pre-war G. Donald Harrison in the 20th, flues were kept open. An ordinary Principal pipe had a flue whose width approximated the metal thickness of the lower lip. Naturally it was also endowed with copious nicking. The tone was often rich but without chiff. Nobody in America worried about nicking until experts of the postwar German "organ reform" pronounced that, for Bach and his predecessors, nicking was *verboten*. In the 1950s American voicers everywhere began trying to do without nicking. They discovered that one got a pleasant "chiff" that way, but also a sustained and most unpleasant frying sound— as of bacon and eggs in the skillet—unless they greatly narrowed the flue. They then found that if they narrowed the flue to a hairline crack they could get rid of the frying sound, but at the cost of a certain boldness and character in the tone. Most American voicers of the 1950s were sensitive to this loss of character but went along with the change toward narrower flues because so many organists were demanding what might be called "the neo-baroque sound," and increasingly were seeking to satisfy their wants with imports. Voicing with narrow flues and very light nicking is common in most American organ shops today.

The trouble is that the German experts' version of the Bach organ was only partly right. True, most organ pipes from Bach's time and before have little or no nicking, but the flues are almost never hairline. Often in old work the flues are as wide as the lip metal thickness, particularly from 1′ pitch upward. These pipes seem able to "have their cake and eat it too." They possess the open-flued boldness and easy character of Hook's and Harrison's best work, yet they speak with the incisiveness that comes from leaving out nicks—all with no eggs frying. How can this be?

Compare a 17th-century pipe to a 20th-century pipe. The new pipe glitters; the old looks up at you dully with sleepy eyes and a yawn. The flue of the new pipe is neatly chiselled as if machine-made; the flue of the old pipe has an acutely distressed look. Moss seems to be growing on the languid; often there are tool marks roughly made in that tenderest of all places, the languid's lower leading edge. In short, the old pipe looks as if its maker just didn't care. Yet its tone and speech belie this notion.

Here in the Fisk workshop we have always worked with open flues. We have done this by using just enough nicking to attenuate the frying sound, meanwhile retaining boldness and a pleasant chiff. To us the tone achieved is good, but it is never quite like the sound of the old organs because the nicking, being itself an artistic ingredient, introduces a certain grainy quality to the tone, a shimmer, sometimes even a silvery quality, that is a specialty in itself. It is this very quality imparted by the nicking that gives Hook's and Harrison's organs some of their particular character.

The question remains: How can we produce sounds as beautiful as the oldest sounds? The answer is elusive, but it surely includes keeping flues open without using nicks—seemingly impossible in a newly made, undistressed organ pipe. Probably the answer also includes the use of the Gegenphase or counter-face (what Cavaillé-Coll calls *la saillie*), which is to be found in literally all of the old work including that of the 19th century, and which consists of an almost microscopic vertical faceting or blunting of the languid's lower leading edge.

But there are no easy answers. If we American organ builders and organists are to learn what the old organs really have to teach us, we should be turning our full attention to this problem of the flues. And we should listen not to whatever doctrine may be currently fashionable but to the musical sounds themselves.

Some Thoughts on Pipe Metal

As I write this, the price of tin hovers around six dollars per pound. Five years ago it was less than three dollars. For organ builders, most of whom tend to feel that their instruments are already too expensive, the rise of tin price has been a throughgoing headache.

Each builder in his own way has sought relief from the tin price problem. Some have shifted upward the breaking point between their zinc basses and their tin alloy trebles. Others have cut their spotted metal from a flashy 52% to the old prewar 42%. Flutes that once were made of spotted metal are now made in common or Hoyt's metal. Polished tin facade pipes, ever a luxury, are now regarded as a shocking extravagance. And some builders are beginning to use 97% lead for a large part of their flue work; these builders are, in effect, turning their backs on tin as a material for organ pipes.

If you look inside an E. M. Skinner organ of the 1920s, you are made aware that in America tin was not always used on the extensive scale we have come to regard as normal. G. Donald Harrison, Ernest Skinner's successor, was the man who started us all on our tin habit, a habit later much intensified by the postwar Dutch, German, Swiss and Danish export builders who often used tin alloys for all bass pipes, thus eliminating zinc entirely from the organ. Nowadays most organists will tell you that tin is good, lead is not, and zinc is something one tries not to talk about. (Most organ builders agree that zinc is primarily a metal of convenience. Large bass pipes made of soft metals like lead and tin are very difficult to handle in the workshop and in transit without denting; zinc has more strength for its weight and produces a very durable pipe.)

But if there is little argument over zinc, the lead versus tin argument cannot be disposed of so easily. Centuries old, it has always had to endure the influence of the cost factor, one aspect of which is the popular assumption that the more expensive metal produces the better sound.

If American organ building, through economic necessity, is headed for more lead, does this mean a loss of quality for America's future instruments? For an answer to this question we should consult history.

Tin has always been an expensive metal, and while it boasts a long history of use in organ building, the fact is that "pure" lead—without any additions whatever—was the normal material for making organ pipes almost up to the time of Schnitger. (By "pure" lead I mean the purest lead available at the time, i.e., a metal which analyzes at around 97% lead and 3% trace metals which the refining process of the time could not remove.) Schnitger rebuilt a great many Gothic and Renaissance organs, and what a scavenger he was! He never threw aside any stop that in his eyes had virtue. We thus find in his organs stop after stop from earlier builders made of "pure" lead. His elegant organ at the Aa Kerk in Groningen retains many old stops, including de Mare's 16, 8 and 4 foot foundations for the Great chorus. These are of "pure" lead and lend a surpassing dignity to Schnitger's instrument. Interestingly enough, Schnitger often saved the lead foundation stops but habitually threw out the lead mixtures he found in the Gothic and Renaissance organs, preferring the *schneidend* quality of his own mixtures, which were usually made with about 20% of tin.

What are the characteristic sounds of the old lead stops? First, a darkness, a hollowness, a sound as of deepest antiquity. Second, an astonishing agility, an ability to move as the music moves, to flit about like a freshly hatched insect. These two characteristics seem contradictory, and indeed, as I see it, the attractiveness of lead pipes seems to lie in the paradox that qualities of youth and great age can cohabit the same mysterious envelope.

Another paradox relates to the strength of the sound. A lead pipe, when voiced in the old way, yields a tone with a softness about it, an unformed, amateurish kind of tone. Yet a chorus of lead pipes produces resultants of great carrying power. Lead is what gave the small Gothic organ the power to fill a vast cathedral. Recall the little organ at Oosthuizen and its "brave sound," as E. Power Biggs so aptly titles it. That bravura, that *all-out* quality, is the sound of lead.

What, alternatively, is the sound of tin? I think of it as the sound of *refinement*, the argentine sound of the French Plein Jeu, or at its very best, the blaze of weightless color and light that Gottfried Silbermann knew so well how to achieve in his paper-thin, hammered tin choruses. Tin pipes love to produce overtones, and there is something about the metal that lends itself to the production of *pleasing* overtones, particularly when the voicing is done in the old way, with high cutups. This is how the "silver" of Silbermann is achieved. In our own time, unfortunately, there has been a widespread tendency to make tin pipes with walls that are thick (a waste of material) and with cutups that are low (a French technique) and with toeholes that are wide open (a German idea). No wonder that upperwork made in this polyglot way is piercing beyond the bounds of music; no wonder that foundations so constructed are foundationless and characterless. Low cutups put the tin in a bad mood, so to speak, whence it cannot rise to its natural elegance. I believe the misapplication and abuse of tin will come to be seen historically as the great organ building mistake of the '50s, '60s, and '70s.

Those Americans wishing to seek out the virtues of lead might appreciate a few reflections on the problems lead presents for the manufacture of organ pipes:

1. Lead is difficult to cast into sheets because of the high temperature

required and because there is no pastey stage as there is in the lead/tin alloys. Casting must be done on a fiberglass or Nomex cloth; cotton or linen will disintegrate.

2. Pig lead available on the market is generally so pure as to be dead soft and must therefore be doctored. By adding some of the impurities that come naturally in the old "pure" lead of the 17th century, the metal can be made sturdy enough to stand for many years. Antimony (0.75%), copper (0.06%), bismuth (0.05%) and tin (1.0%) when added all together will produce the desired stiffening. Curiously, lead with these trace elements scarcely creeps at all; ordinary common metal (20% tin, 80% lead) creeps far more. This explains why the lead front pipes from the Gothic and Renaissance stand without any sign of collapsing, while American common metal front pipes of the early 19th century always sagged. Adding tin to the lead actually *increases* the creep. (For this information our whole trade is indebted to Herman Greunke, organ curator at the Oberlin Conservatory of Music, who is a learned source on the subject of lead technology as applied to organs.)

3. The tone seems best when the metal is hammered. When cast, 97% lead is particularly porous. It seems not to be hardened by hammering, but it *is* made more dense, and this is apparently helpful. Cavaillé-Coll says, "Hammering renders the metal more dense and more sonorous." Cor Edskes maintains that hammering causes the pipes to speak more quickly.

4. Lead pipes require less nicking than do tin-alloy pipes, particularly if there is a small counterface (Gegenphase) on the leading edge of the languid.

5. Scales that are right for tin or spotted metal will be too large for lead. A lead stop should be two to three scales smaller than its tin-alloy counterpart. People have often wondered at the slender scales of the front pipes in Dutch and German cases of the Renaissance. These scales were correct for lead, and the organs they served were by no means the bass-hungry devices we might imagine them to be.

6. It is useless to try for an edgy or stringy sound from "pure" lead. Not that it is impossible; indeed, a low cutup mouth sharply skived will produce a surprising array of overtones. But it is as if the pipe were saying to the voicer, "All right, I'll do it your way, but you aren't going to like it." There is something heavy and unpleasant about the overtones thus forced from lead. The solution is to cut the pipe up until the mouth is no longer imposing its will on the resonator and the tone is relatively free of "mouth engendered" overtones. A lead mixture pipe when cut up high enough sounds a little like a traverse flute, especially when blown by mouth.

Returning to Cambridge after one of his many European trips, the late E. Power Biggs was heard to say, "There must be at least a dozen ways of building an absolutely perfect organ." This brings to mind Landowska's famous pronouncement, "In art there is no progress—only change." Clearly, an organ's artistic merit does not depend on whether its builder uses lead or tin for his pipes but on *how* he uses what he uses. It is a simple question, really: If American organ builders wish to rely more on lead than they have in the past, let them consider the masterful examples set by the de Mares and Schnitgers of our world, and then let them apply their own unbiased ears and their own immutable good taste.

How Certain Musical Differences between the Historic Organs of Germany and France were Achieved by Differences in Construction

It's a curious turn of fate that brings scholarly interest in the organ to its present state. That the love of Bach's music should bring us to study antique Dutch and German organs—most of which Bach never heard—and that a still-alive tradition resting squarely on Cavaillé-Coll should indirectly fill us with yearning for the French Classic Organ—these are quirks of musical history we can only marvel at. And that all this overlies some two centuries of English domination of New World organ practice? Curious indeed! Beneath, of course, lies one simple fact: we North Americans are musical omnivores, eclecticists. If anything sounds good—or sounded good once upon a time—we want to be able to hear it.

This year, for the first time, four organ builders from Canada and the United States are completing organs which are virtual copies of instruments built three hundred years ago in Europe. Strange that such an event occurs only now, considering that we have been barking up this tree since 1932. And yet we cannot be surprised by this if we remember that a whole continent's interest has had to be brought along, step by step, through a thousand gradations of eclecticism to the present state of academic near-purity.

I feel sure that we North Americans will never be able to abandon eclecticism entirely. It's such a fascinating game to try to make an organ do more than anybody thought it would. And I have to confess that in my recent studies and imitatings of the two model organs that concern me in this lecture—the French Classic Organ and the North German Organ of the 17th century—I have never given up the notion that I might be led to a better understanding of how better eclectic organs might be built.

Even as late as the 17th century, three hundred years after the Blockwerk began to be broken up into separate stops, the organs of Germany and France still had many things in common. They had wooden cases that were never very deep, enclosed on all sides but the front, always with front pipes taken from the largest stops, and almost always with carved wooden fretwork to close in the spaces above and below the front pipes, thereby helping the front pipes discourage egress of the highest pitched overtones from inside the case. All had note-channel windchests, mostly of the pallet and slider type. They were tracker organs employing wooden traces, levers, squares, and rollers to connect keyboards to windchests. A bank of two or more cuneiform bellows, usually planted a short distance behind the organ, provided air to a single plenum wind duct seldom larger than a foot square in section. This single trunk, often about 20 feet long, ran from the bellows into the organ case and there divided like the branches of a tree, each branch smaller in section than the main trunk and each ending in the pallet box of a windchest.

Since the aforementioned elements comprise what one first sees upon looking into any old organ, a natural reaction is that there must be a great similarity in the tonal effect of all old organs. But, as we know, this is not really true. To discuss the differences we must begin with the cultural bases for our two models.

To be French is French and to be German is German. To be French in the late 1600s was to serve a king, to love delicacy and refinement, to prefer the exquisite in all things gentle, and in things bold to love the sounds of a highly organized military, the unmatchable vibrancy and éclat of omnipotence. To be successfully French was to maintain a control, a savoir faire.

But to be a North German, in say, 1650, just after the Thirty Years War? This was to serve either a town council or local nobility, to live close to the land or close to the sea, to be Protestant. And in all things Protestant, there must have been a highly developed sense of Life's paradoxes: the loftiness of God and the nearness of God, the beauty of life at its best and the horror at its worst, the drudgery of now and the joy of the heavenly hereafter. In one glance they always seemed to see the light and the darkness intertwined. Dignity and savior faire are less important in this German world where God, Magistrate, Burger and Bauer were all part of one well-regulated family, and the sounds they loved were those of people dancing and singing, and, in their imaginations, the dancing, singing, and—occasionally—the thundering of the heavenly hosts.

The French Classic Organ is a grande dame of greatest beauty, poise, refinement and temperament, somewhat distant and unapproachable, but capable of charming anyone in her realm. The North German Organ is a plain-faced girl in a dirndl who jumps up and asks you to dance.

Now down to the rock bottom of technical detail that reflects these character differences. Looking first at the flue chorus, it is well known that raw lead was for years the standard material for pipemaking in North Germany, whereas in France the admixture of tin to lead was adopted at an early time. Raw lead is a plain-sounding material that imparts no marked overtone structure to the tone of a pipe, whereas tin adds a sheen of overtones which, under the right circumstances, produces a tone of explicit elegance. Moreover, tin imparts its sheen even when the pipes are gently blown, thus lending a special serenity and majesty to the French Plein Jeu, which tended to be less than full blown. So used, tin is thus the metal of refinement and delicacy. As for lead: if lead pipes are gently blown, they produce a tone of no particular distinction. Lead comes alive only when it is blown full. Assuming cutups that are high enough to avoid edginess, the tone of a chorus of lead pipes blown full is deceptively massive, with resultant tones that give a marked solidity to the fundamental. There is a faint halo of overtones that imparts a human or naturalistic flavor. Perhaps the most wonderful characteristic of lead pipes, both principals and flutes, is the agility they seem to give an organ. Lead pipes reach their note so quickly, firmly, and gracefully that they will clearly delineate even a disjunct sixteenth-note figure in the lower register. Lead pipes and the type of voicing they encourage are largely responsible for the open-faced "let's dance" quality that is so much a part of the North German Organ. The face of lead is the face of the girl in the dirndl; but the tone of lead is dark—much darker, incidentally, than the thin tone of the modern Neo-Baroque organs, most of which disregard totally the essential paradox of the North German Baroque, the paradox so often expressed in the old case pipes of black lead trimmed in filaments of gold, again: the paradox of darkness versus light.

The difference of character between things French and German is nowhere more evident than in the reed stops, and especially in the treatment of the organ trumpet stops.

Organ reed pipes consist of two parts, the motor and the resonator. The motor, which contains the block, shallot, tongue, and tuning wire, corresponds to the mouthpiece and embouchure of an orchestral wind instrument, while the resonator corresponds to the "horn" held in the player's hands. If you ask a wind player to detach the mouthpiece from his instrument and blow through it, the results are squawks, squeaks, and buzzing—the raw stuff from which wind instrument sound is always made. In an organ reed pipe, detaching the resonator from the motor produces similar noises, except that the buzzes sound more metallic, owing to the vibrating parts being made of brass instead of cane or human flesh. Quite evidently, in wind instruments the resonator's job is to render harmonious the raw sound energy produced by the motor, but this is a job of varying difficulty depending on the relative roughness or smoothness of the motor's output. Indeed, the tremendous variety of tone possible in organ trumpet stops is largely owing to different designs of motor, especially since the resonator always has the same shape, namely that of an inverted cone.

The critical elements of the motor are the curved brass tongue and the shallot against which it is made to beat by the force of the surrounding air. Trumpet pipes from the Renaissance employed a thin tongue and a single wide-open brass shallot with a very narrow rim for the tongue to beat against. The throat, i.e., the upper end of the shallot through which the air passes on into the resonator, was generous. The tone of pipes made in this way is loud, brilliant, and rather metallic, especially in the bass. Indeed, there is a marked tendency for the bass of such a trumpet to drown out its own treble. Wide-open

Renaissance shallots produce such a blaze of overtones in bass pipes that the darker and thinner sounding treble pipes merely seem to become part of the bass pipe structure and have no melodic life of their own. Such a trumpet is, of course, ideal for lining out a cantus firmus in the tenor or bass, and it is thrilling in chords and fanfares. But taken by itself, the Renaissance Trumpet is of little use in complex polyphony.

Historically, a great deal of thought has gone into devising ways of getting around the tendency of the trumpet bass to dominate the trumpet treble. For the orchestral trumpeter, too, this would be a problem were it not for his ability to apply much greater air pressure for his high notes than for his low notes. Indeed, the 19th century organ builder, Cavaillé-Coll, chose precisely this orchestral solution: he simply placed his treble pipes on higher chest pressure than his bass pipes. Other solutions exist, as we shall see.

A second problem area for organ trumpet stops centers around the combining of trumpets with choruses of flue pipes. Reeds and flues produce their tones according to two totally different physical principles, so perhaps we should only marvel that they can be used in combination at all. The crucial difference lies in the attack: flue pipes—even those with a transient chiff—begin their notes relatively gently and on time; the trumpet, however, begins its notes explosively, and often a bit "late," depending on the amount of tongue curvature. The initial explosion is occasioned, of course, by the inrushing air which slams the tongue shut flat against the shallot, much as a gust of wind will slam a door in an open house in summer. This first stroke of the tongue is followed by others, and there ensues a short period of musically important confusion, during which the resonator, so to speak, wakes up and realizes that it must rouse itself and join the tongue in its jubilations. The vibrations heard during the period of confusion constitute the reed pipe's version of the chiff—its signature. Signature is a useful word here because every reed pipe has its own unique way of beginning its note, a pattern of vibrations unlike those of any other reed pipe. The signatures of pipes of the Renaissance Trumpet family are the "John Hancocks" of the organ world. Brassy, effusive, spectacular, they rivet the attention. The horizontal trumpets of Spain and Portugal are the best remaining examples of the Renaissance Trumpet; by their appearance and their clattering, they unmistakably suggest the many-tiered guns of a Spanish galleon. There is an "all-out" quality here that cannot be matched by flue work of any kind.

French bon goût did not allow the French Classic Organ to retain quite the all-out quality so loved by the Spaniards; nevertheless, the French let the assembled trumpets take the responsibility for creating the French Classic Organ's most formidable effect, the Grand Jeu. Further, to make the treble line heard above the trumpet basses, they added the Cornet de dessus, a compound stop of five flue ranks (including the tierce) voiced and scaled to expand markedly in power as it approached the treble. And the French Trumpet is essentially the Renaissance Trumpet, somewhat refined by scaling down the shallots and resonator tips, and by never allowing it outside the organ case. Hammered tin was used for the trumpet resonators to intensify the overtones, and thin tongues beating against thin-rimmed shallots gave to the whole array the signatures of splendor and éclat. When the trumpets are drawn in a French organ it is as though the organ has become angry. But dignity, breadth, equanimity, serenity, pathos—these are mainly provinces of the fluework which is always held back to an extent in its winding, as if to avoid encroaching on the territory of the trumpets.

Cor Edskes says that about 1550 the Scherers of Hamburg adopted a new form of bass shallot representing a total departure from the simple shallot of the Renaissance. The habit of using these new shallots for trumpet basses, and for all reed basses except those of the regals, rapidly took over in the coastal areas of Germany and the Netherlands, where their use has never been completely discontinued. These shallots have wide bores and correspondingly wide tongues, but between the tongue and the shallot opening is soldered a heavy lead plate—in effect, a cover for the shallot opening. The center of this lead plate is pierced with an elongated hole occupying about one-third of the plate area; through this hole the air flows into the shallot and thence into the resonator. In Schnitger's organs the lead plate is usually surfaced with leather; earlier builders were ambivalent about the use of leather for the shallot surface.

An obvious function of the lead plate is to limit the flow of sound energy passing through the shallot. Because the plate is made of lead, it is easy with a knife to enlarge the elongated hole; this gives the voicer control of the amount of sound energy passing into the resonator, and therefore the opportunity to adjust the loudness of the bass pipes relative to the treble pipes, which have no lead plate. Moreover, the effect of cutting down the energy of the bass pipes by limiting the hole size also diminishes overtones and makes the steady-state tone not only gentle but muffled, rather like the tone of an orchestral French Horn. This is a far cry from the splashy trumpet of the Renaissance, but it is a trumpet which blends very nicely with the flue chorus.

A second and equally important function of the lead plate is to speed up and intensify the attack. Consider the shallot and tongue in the rest position: the tongue is poised close above the lead plate. When air is suddenly admitted to the system, its only escape is through the elongated hole and into the shallot, but its path takes it through the narrow zone between the tongue and the unpierced portion of the lead plate. In such a narrows, the air velocity rises, and where velocity rises, pressure drops, as we know by Bernouilli's principle—the famous principle that accounts for the lift of an airplane wing. The combination of the energizing positive pressure above and Bernouilli's negative pressure (suction) beneath the tongue causes it to slam shut with much more force than would be the case without the lead plate. Trumpet basses using these shallots actually speak more quickly than flue basses of the same pitch and are thus ideal for assisting the flue choruses in rapid passage work. Indeed, in an organ with pedal towers mounted on the gallery railing, as at the Cosmaekirche in Stade, the effect of the pedal trumpets is positively percussive: a rapid pedal trill in a low register produces the illusion of two tuned drums being beaten in oscillatory fashion. That the brass tongues are broad and thick, and that they beat against a heavy lead plate covered with animal skin, undoubtedly contributes to this illusion, as does the fact that the slamming of tongue against shallot telegraphs throughout the organ framework and the entire balcony structure.

One cannot talk about the reeds in a German organ without mentioning their influence on other pipes via the note channel, the tunnel-like chamber in the windchest which fills with air when the key corresponding to it is depressed and which, in turn, feeds air to all the pipes on the chest that correspond to the key.

Now it is well known that any sounding organ pipe sends a portion of its sound energy back through its own foot into the note channel. When several pipes over the same note channel are sounding, the aggregate of their sound within the note channel can be very intense. This is especially true when reed pipes are sounding. One strong reed pipe can set up vibrations in a note channel that will compel all the flue pipes on the channel to "fall into line," i.e., to synchronize their pitches with harmonics of the reed. Furthermore, if the reed pipe is of low pitch relative to its channel-neighbor flue pipes, for example a sixteen-foot Pedal Posaune speaking on the same channel with a mixture—each small flue pipe will "flutter" or warble in sympathy with the flapping of the Posaune's tongue, and in so doing will become secondary sources of the Posaune's tonal output. Indeed, even though the Posaune produces, out of its own resonator, a smooth, foundational sound, the fluttering heard in the flue chorus belies this smoothness; instead, the fluttering seems to comprise mainly upper harmonics in the Posaune that would pass unnoticed if the Posaune were sounding alone. In this way the Posaune's natural darkness is embroidered with a light of its own making, thanks to the intermediation of the flue work.

The North German Trumpet may have had the steady-state tone of a muffled horn and the signature of a muffled drum, but it could set the flue work ablaze. In fact, the sound of flues and reeds drawn together in a big German organ has some of the angry quality of the French Grand Jeu, due largely to the reeds' acting upon the upper work via the note channels.

Ah, the note channel—what mysteries lie hidden in that small medieval tunnel! Organ sound is conceived in the note channel, born in the pipe. Half the troubles in an organ seem to originate in the note channel, and yet, so also do a thousand unknowable, dissertation-worthy intricacies that help make of the organ the instrument we find so irresistible.

    It was German to be obsessed with the possibilities the note channel brought to the art of combining stops on the same windchest. It was French, however, to wish for a more reasonable note channel, one with fewer mysteries—and fewer problems. The classic French builders used, therefore, a note channel that leaks its sound away through a flexible leather membrane on its underside, thereby freeing each pipe to act more on its own, with less interference from its channel neighbors. Not until Cavaillé-Coll do we see in France hard-walled note channels again put to signal use: he found that by placing his choruses of Bombardes over small, tight note channels he could create those doomsday throbbings, those wondrous sounds that seem to be coming from some great buzzsaw in the sky.

UNPUBLISHED ARTICLES AND TALKS

The Spanish Baroque Organ in Mexico Cathedral

[*Editor's note: In 1953, while still living in California, Charles Fisk and a college friend, Robert McAfee, went on an "organ crawl" to Mexico. There they saw a number of antique instruments—most of them unplayable—which in fact constituted Fisk's first exposure to historic old-world organ building practices. This article, written upon his return, records young Fisk's reactions to one of the organs in Mexico City Cathedral before its later damage by fire and eventual restoration. Unfortunately the article was never finished or published, and, save for the first three pages, had to be reconstructed from a partially handwritten draft.*]

ONE OF THE MOST SERIOUS IMPEDIMENTS to the success of the *Orgelreform* in America has been the lack of even one classical instrument which might serve as a model for study. If we accept, sound unheard, the hypothesis that the finest organs were built prior to 1780, then we must conclude that American organ builders have been at a dreadful disadvantage in trying to reproduce these fine old instruments. This is particularly true in the light of European builders' difficulties even when they had the prototypes at hand. American organ builders have thus had to work from "glimpses" of classical European organs, meanwhile trying to indoctrinate an audience which, until the advent of the most recent phonograph recordings, had never been able to *hear* a truly classical organ, not to say appreciate it.

The dearth of classic prototypes on our own continent, however, is probably not as extreme as many people believe. We need only to look to Mexico to find them. Most Americans are comfortably unaware of the cultural seniority held by the Spanish-settled areas of the new world. In Mexico, the full impact of western culture was felt instantly upon the arrival of Cortez—this a hundred years before the Pilgrims "infiltrated" at Plymouth. Thus, in Mexico, one occasionally finds churches which were built in the Renaissance, while baroque churches and cathedrals are everywhere. Since many of these buildings undoubtedly held organs, it stands to reason that there still exist quite a few classic organs in Mexico.

Probably the two most imposing classical instruments in all the hemisphere are in the gigantic Cathedral at Mexico City. The authors were privileged to spend a day and a half examining these organs, in the spring of 1953. The examination was undertaken without preparation—without even a wind gauge—but with the aid of a good stereoscopic camera, which answered many of the questions which arose later. We shall presently attempt to describe one of the two organs in detail.

Mexico Cathedral is built in the normal cruciform fashion of Spanish colonial churches, but is unusual because of its three-sided choir screen, placed on the center of the nave. The two organs, almost identical in appearance, are built upon the two parallel side walls of this screen, and face each other across the choir enclosure. But they also face outward upon the side aisles of the nave; thus each organ has two parallel façades, inner and outer, choir and nave. Each organ has a Ruckpositiv at the foot of its inner (choir) façade; the organist sits in the usual position between the Ruckpositiv and the main organ. Just above the organist's head, and within his reach, are five ranks of reed *en chamade*. Larger chamade reeds project from the nave façade and extend awning-wise over the heads of passersby. The chamades add the final flourish to the casework, which, with its eloquent carving and perfect proportion, is the glowing fulfillment of the baroque ideal.

In his book, *Baroque and Rococo in Latin America* (Macmillan), Mr. Pal Keleman gives interesting historical facts about the organs of Mexico Cathedral. According to his account the epistle organ was built in Spain, while the gospel organ was built later in Mexico. (The organs are so much alike, both inside and out, that one must have been copied from the other.) The request to Spain for the Spanish organ is dated 1688; we have been unable to discover exactly when this instrument was completed, although the inscription "1696" appears on the archway just below it. Both organs were dedicated in 1736.

We chose to limit our detailed observations to the Spanish organ. We found it to consist of three independent divisions: a Great, a Choir, and a Pedal. These are controlled by two manuals, each of 50 notes compass, CC, DD–d_3, and but ten pedal notes, CCC, DDD, EEE–BBB, i.e., one short octave. The manual keys are similar to our own; even the spacing between the two manuals is not far from A.G.O. standard. The pedals, widely spaced, protrude only five inches out of the kickboard. These ten little pedals are duplicated by a short octave of ten manual pulldown keys placed just to the left of the Great (upper) manual. There are no couplers. Far to the right of the manuals is an additional 27 note keyboard which plays a small echo organ.

Both manual departments of the organ are divided uniformly into half stops, in the manner of a reed organ. All bass half stops are controlled by draw knobs to the left of the keyboards, while treble half stops are drawn on the right. For all stops the break between bass and treble occurs between middle C and C#. About half of the stops in the organ run the full gamut, that is, have a matching bass and treble; the remainder are different in bass and treble. For example, none of the Cornets have bass counterparts; they are all simply treble half stops, proceeding upwards from c#$_1$. The division of the organ into half stops greatly increases its flexibility, and saves the organ builder from having to make expensive and wind consuming basses for some of the low-pitched large scale treble stops.

The physical layout of the organ is extraordinarily simple, which is partly responsible for an extreme lightness of touch on both manuals. The Choir organ, controlled by the lower manual, is in reality divided into a Brustwerk of 7 full stops and a Ruckpositiv of 3 full stops. The chests of both rest flat upon the floor—the Ruckpositiv just behind the organist, the Brustwerk in front of him, i.e., inside, directly under the main organ. But there are no trackers under the floor to the Ruckpositiv. Instead, the Choir pallet box is located "upside down" on the floor directly below the keyboards and each note of the Brustwerk and Ruckpositiv is tubed from the pallet box; the tubes to the Ruckpositiv run under the organist, while those to the Brustwerk run further inside the organ. A very interesting expansion-chamber situation exists here, due to the large capacity of the tubing plus two normal slider chest key chambers. We noticed that the Ruckpositiv Fifteenth (*Quincena Clara*), a small, unnicked diapason of scale CC(8′) ca. 50, spoke quickly and with a slight but extremely pleasant chiff. When we carefully tried to blow pipes of this stop by mouth, they spoke a steady note only after the most prolonged transient disturbance. The speech regulation of this stop when on the chest was remarkably even.

The Great organ is much larger than the combined Choir. It is composed of four separate slider chests; two hold the 23 treble half stops (above middle C) while the other two hold the 27 bass half stops (below middle C). All four chests are mounted over the Brustwerk just above the organist's head level and they occupy a space the full depth of the organ (about ten feet), so that both console and nave chamades emanate approximately from the chests themselves. The ranks of the Great are arranged in orderly fashion; beginning with the 16′ manual flue nearest the console, and working down to the mixtures on the far side. The Great pallet box is located directly above the keyboards, beneath the manual double; the wind from the pallets must therefore run the full ten foot depth of the organ via the key chambers to reach the mixtures.

The pipework of the organ has a sameness about it that one does not find in a modern organ. All the metal pipes, from the smallest down to the 16 foot fronts, are made of plain metal. There is, however, very little evidence that the pipes have sagged under their own weight. Pipe walls are on the thin side—about the same as in some of Roosevelt's upperwork. All open metal pipes are tuned by either crumpling in or tearing open the upper ends, which gives the pipework a very disheveled appearance, but probably does not greatly affect the speech. All the mouths are cut across square; there are no arched mouths in the organ, and there is no skiving or dubbing of the upper lips. Neither are there any ears, except on a few wooden stops, and on covered stops, where they are the sole means of tuning (the caps of all metal covered stops are simply soldered on, a system which certainly obviates any worry over loose stoppers).

[Note: Either the article was never completed, or some further descriptive pages may be missing here. The paragraphs which follow were found in the same file; they may be the conclusion to this article, or part of another fragmentary article on the same subject.]

Of all the organs to be found in the western hemisphere, those of the Cathedral of Mexico are among the most glorious. They stem from a culmination of grandeur such as has been seen only once in the New World.

On entering the portals of the magnificent cathedral, any person is struck immediately by the authority of the two flamboyant baroque organ cases, with trompettes en chamade. It is interesting for the layman to realize that the authority of these organs is not limited to the casework. Although they are no longer used, thorough examination has shown that these are both mighty instruments capable of sonorities which would rival those of the finest modern organs. Due to the accumulation of dust, their true sonority has probably not been heard for a hundred years.

[The organs] of Mexico Cathedral are almost the only true examples of baroque organ building in this hemisphere. They are thus a very important source of information for "American" organ builders and musicologists. For instance, examination shows that the Spanish baroque organ builders used certain artistic techniques in pipe voicing which were never used by German or French builders. These would be well worth investigating.

Finally, it is fervently to be hoped that these old Patriarchs will one day *speak again*.

[Note: Charles Fisk's hopes for the Mexico City Cathedral organs were, happily, realized during his lifetime; both instruments were restored in 1977 by D. A. Flentrop.]

Articulateness and the Organ: A Problem for the Organ Builder

Lecture given at the dedication of the Flentrop Organ,
Duke University, November 1976

"SOMEDAY people will realize that the organ is a keyboard instrument and not just a big vat of sound." These words were from 1954. They were spoken by Walter Holtkamp, Senior, a man who labored hard to make them come true.

Most of what I have learned about organs has come from working on organs or from observing organs. But I have had two principal teachers. The first was *John Swinford* of Redwood City, California. He taught me about organ tone. The second was *Walter Holtkamp, Sr.* He taught me that an organ should be articulate above everything else. And he did a fair job of teaching this lesson to the country as a whole. Articulateness is something American organ builders now understand and even achieve, whenever architecture permits. As for good tone... well, I think America has forgotten more than it has learned about tone. Sometimes I think both America and Europe have sacrificed good tone to achieve articulateness. Anyone who knows the best of the old organs knows that *that* sacrifice was not necessary—one *can* have both.

But when we talk about *articulateness* in America, we are talking about a kind of success story, a *partial* success story, at any rate. Now, what do I *mean* by articulateness? Well, any small instrument heard close to is articulate. Think of a music box or a clavichord. If everyone is very quiet, it is possible, by listening carefully, to hear every stroke, every vibration, every tiny clunk, thud or whir in the mechanism. This is the very definition of articulateness: to be able to hear and comprehend every sound, every utterance made by the source. Articulateness depends more on the careful handling of high frequencies than of low frequencies. It implies a kind of "close miking"—the familiar result of hanging the microphone so close that the listener imagines he is almost inside the source.

My use of the microphone analogy is premeditated. For, is it only coincidence that our generation's passion for clarity in musical performance parallels the coming of the radio and the phonograph? I think not. It was the close miking of the nineteen-thirties that first put articulate musical performance within reach of all ears. Notice, too, this was the era of jazz and swing on radio and phonograph. Consider how the swing arrangements of the thirties, recorded in the driest acoustics, depended for their effect on the precise electro-acoustical renderings of snare drum rim shots, of syncopated squirts of sound from the large-bore, fast speaking trumpets and saxes employed by the jazz men. Indeed, consider just how much the *saxophone* owes to the radio and phonograph. You may say it sounds like an unwell cow and be right, but the saxophone boasts a *wieldiness*, an articulateness, that is uncanny. It can *move*. And its ability to move is most clearly manifest in a close-miked recording in which the listener, in effect, sits right alongside the performer, sways with the music, and cherishes every golden grunt of that glittering, colon-shaped cornucopia.

Now the organ is a very different kind of an instrument from the saxophone. Some have argued that the organ is *at bottom* an inarticulate musical instrument. What other instrument employs a separate oscillator (i.e., pipe) for every note and for every timbre it produces? (And many of the pipes are larger than the largest saxophone—why, a single pipe can weigh a thousand pounds and more!) The organ's entire effect is based on an almost cancerous proliferation of oscillators, tens of thousands of them. A nightmare I sometimes have involves trying to find my way out of a castle. There are doors leading everywhere. Each time I open a door I peer in on yet *another* room full of windchests with mean looking organ pipes standing on them. Dreams like this have far too much basis in fact, in the haunted houses and churches of 20th-century America.

How can such a multi-chambered instrument—such a *dinosaur* of an instrument—gather itself together for a concerted musical lunge at anything? How can such an organ *organize* itself, mobilize itself for concerted action? By what irony of semantics comes so *dis*organized an instrument to be known as an *Organ*? Should it not be called a *Dis-organ*?

Many a Disorgan has been built within the present century, as we all know, and it was this particular prehistoric beast that Walter Holtkamp rode out to slay some forty years ago.

Let us now look at organ history. Most of the earliest organs would have been articulate simply because they were small. Some surely had the quality of a music box. But the churches were large, and with the Reformation came congregational singing for which large organs were needed. The organ builders of those days included many brilliant and gifted men. By the end of the 16th century these men had in effect *created* the large organ as we know it today. What is truly remarkable, they devised ways of making an organ of sixty stops articulate, as well as beautiful of tone. Furthermore, *nothing* contributed after the 16th century made any improvement whatever in the articulate quality of the organ as an instrument.... In what follows, therefore, I would like to give my interpretation of the methods these wise men chose to achieve articulateness in the organ. I will dwell less on those methods which are commonly understood today, more on those which are not.

We all know about "Chiff." It is the little incise or transient that an organ pipe gives out naturally when it begins its tone. The basic Principal organ pipe "chiffs" if its windway is lightly nicked or not nicked at all. More and more nicking diminishes the chiff until finally it becomes inaudible. The chiff sounds like "KAA..." and sometimes "CHAA..." or even "SHAA...." With too little wind it takes on a tubercular quality, a kind of cough. In E. Power Biggs's words, the chiff is the consonant that precedes the vowel. Using his metaphor it is easy to show that the chiff, or something like it, is essential to articulateness—for: Who ever heard of articulation without consonants? Some form of chiff was present in all the early organs.

I now wish to introduce what I believe to be a new viewpoint. Always we have thought of an organ pipe simply as a device for making musical tone, an end in itself. Always we have thought of all other parts of the organ as simply being there to serve the pipe. What if we now turn around and consider the pipe the servant of what lies beneath it? What if we now say that a vital function of the organ pipe is that of sensing and converting into audible pulses the air pulses that enter its toe hole? In other words, we are going to think of the organ pipe as a *transducer* of *air* pulses into *sound* pulses. For those who understand the principles of radio, we are thinking of the organ pipe as providing a carrier wave which will be modulated by whatever air pulses may enter the toe hole.

Suppose I blow an organ pipe by mouth and I tongue it, like a trumpeter: "Ta, ta, ta." An ideal principal pipe tongued in this fashion will somehow tell us that it is being tongued using an initial "T." I can next blow the same pipe using the letter "K": "Ka, ka, ka." The ideal pipe will now begin its note in a slightly different way, somehow letting us know that the letter "K" was involved in initiating the pulse of air instead of the letter "T."

In a similar way the ideal pipe can tell us how an air pulse *terminates*. The pulse "TAAAT" sounds different from the pulse "KAAAK." (Also we can tell the difference between "TAAAK" and "KAAAT.") From this we see that the ideal pipe can give us all sorts of information about the way pulses of air coming through the toe hole begin and terminate.

We have talked about the beginning and ending of the tone. What about the part in the middle; what can the pipe tell us? Well, we know, for example, that the regular air pulses produced by the tremulant are "recorded" by the pipe in the form of alternating surgings and ebbings of pitch, volume and harmonic output—a wave motion which, at its worst, can make us slightly seasick! Much more important, actually, is the pipe's habit of recording—i.e., transducing—*irregular* surges of air coming into its foot, because in *these* surges is contained the information *by which the ear perceives clusters of pipes as unities*, and this is of course crucial for the articulateness we seek.

Those of you who know about the voicing of organ pipes will have been put on edge by my use of the term "ideal principal pipe" in the above. By this I mean *a classically voiced pipe*, but this implies a good deal more than just that there be a few nicks in the windway. John Swinford used to say, "A pipe always sounds best when it is a little underblown." All the classical organ builders knew this, yet it is a fact largely disregarded by the present day proponents of the neo-baroque in organ building. Let me try to explain what I mean by underblowing: If you first agree that the windway must be kept open (almost the width of the material of the lower lip) and that there will be enough nicking or "antiquing" of the languid edge to rid us of the unpleasant sizzle that the open windway otherwise causes, then classical voicing becomes a matter of balancing the toe hole opening and the cutup (i.e., the height of the mouth opening). If we choose a wide open toe hole, then underblowing will be achieved if we raise the cutup *just beyond* the point at which the pipe appears to be giving out its maximum volume of sound. Thus the classically voiced organ pipe is one in which the cutup is "a little too high." With the cutup on the high side, the tone becomes fuller and gentler; more important, the pipe is not quite as stable as it would be with a lower cutup, and this makes it *much* more easily influenced by pulses or irregularities in the flow of air coming through its toe hole.

Let me indulge in an analogy that will be close to the heart of all church musicians. The ideal pipe—this classically voiced pipe—can be likened to an ideal member of a chorus of *human* voices. Obviously it is no *prima donna*. Nor is it your average solo coloratura, hired to drown out the volunteer voices in the village choir. Rather, it is a somewhat *insecure* voice that looks to the other voices around it for substantiation in both pitch and diction. It is a bit of a white-toned voice, too, one that blends very well. And, to carry the analogy one step further, the ideal pipe *watches the conductor like a hawk*, since in my analogy the conductor is the pallet valve, controlling the wind to all pipes of a given note.

So far I have talked about a single pipe. What about its relationship to other pipes?

For more than a thousand years (discounting the first half of this century) it has been customary to connect each key of the keyboard, via sticks and wires known as trackers, to a *single valve*. For discussion, let us choose a note, say treble C—the C above middle C. Like all others', treble C's pallet valve is normally shut, and thus holds back the ever ready chest air from flowing into the treble C *note channel*. The note channel is a kind of corridor connecting the pallet valve hole to toe holes of all treble C pipes, of which there might be 30 or 40 in a large organ.

When we depress treble C's key, the treble C pallet valve opens and air surges into the treble C note channel. Immediately air starts into the treble C pipes, and they commence to sound. After some initial bobbing about, the pressure in the note channel stabilizes at virtually the same pressure as is in the wind chest, and remains so as long as we hold the key down. When we release the key the pallet shuts vigorously, residual compressed air drains out through the pipes, and all treble C pipes become mute until their services are required again.

Picture a cluster of 30 or 40 ideal treble C pipes, each pipe highly sensitive to the pressure fluctuations beneath it, all standing over a common note channel, waiting quietly for the wind. The finger presses, the pallet begins to open; all pipes now execute their chiffs in unison. The note channel pressure rises jaggedly up to and momentarily past its stable value; the combined wails from all pipes also rise jaggedly up to and past their stable values, in unison, like a Greek chorus (only more perfect). The pressure now settles back down to its stable value, and the pipes descend to the pitch/volume/timbre that they give out in their "normal" valve-open sounding position. While they are still sounding, there occur fluctuations in the chest pressure, caused by other musical happenings deep inside the organ; these fluctuations are "recorded" by all pipes of our cluster simultaneously as variations in the pitch/volume/timbre of the note they are sounding. Now, finally, the valve begins to shut. As the valve nears its closed position, the air rushing through it drives it shut with a slam, just like a slamming door. This final slamming of the valve drives a final pulse of air through the pipes that momentarily raises the note-channel pressure above anything heretofore experienced, and our cluster records that fact with the highest values of pitch/volume/timbre yet experienced. Immediately thereafter the pressure in the note channel falls away rapidly and the wail of the cluster subsides into silence.

Can you now see how singularly important to the articulateness of the classical organ are the *single pallet* and the *single note channel?* For, *whatever the form* of the pressure fluctuations in the treble C note channel, *all* treble C pipes give out the *same message* about these fluctuations, and this fact tricks the human ear into regarding them as the work of but *one voice*. It is as if the choir director in our previous analogy could, with only his fingers, control the flow of air through the larynxes of all his sopranos simultaneously! Imagine how precisely his sopranos would attack, release, crescendo and diminuendo if the director possessed such a power! He would have the most articulate choir in Christendom.

We have discussed the single note, or pipe-cluster, treble C and how it can become a unity, capable of the articulateness of a single voice. What now of its relationship to other notes, other pipe clusters?

Imagine we are sustaining our old friend, the soprano note treble C, and, simultaneously, the alto note, *middle* C. Now let the alto voice move stepwise upward to middle D (all the while we are sustaining treble C). What change do we observe in the soprano note while the alto is in process of moving?

In the classical organ the slamming of the middle C valve causes a surge in the chest pressure. This is followed immediately by a drop in chest pressure due to the opening of the middle D valve. These two pulses, the first positive, the second negative, are minutely transduced into sound pulses by the continuously sounding treble C cluster. Thus, treble C, by not remaining absolutely constant in pitch/volume/timbre, is making a *little announcement* that there occurred a movement in another voice. In the contrapuntal music written for the classical organ this type of little announcement represents an enormous clarification for the ear. In a six voice fugue, if one voice moves while the other five sustain, there will be five simultaneous little announcements from the five sustaining voices "pointing to" the motion of the moving voice. Under these circumstances the listener is able to keep track of the motion of inner parts, even with all stops drawn and even with reverberant acoustics.

The classical organ builders made these little announcements possible by designing wind systems which were susceptible to slight fluctuations of pressure whenever the demand for air changed. The *average* value of the pressure was always constant, however. For modern organ building this subject, known as Flexible Winding, is still a controversial one, because it is so natural to assume that the air pressure in an organ must always be imperturbably constant, even though in fact it never is.

I hope it is clear from all of the foregoing that enormous importance attaches to the design of the "chassis" of the organ, if clarity is to be achieved. I feel that not nearly enough attention has been paid to the problems of the bellows, the dimensions of wind ducts, of pallet boxes, of note-channels—the whole air system that represents the matrix for the pipes. In a real sense, every organ is "cushioned on air." How does that cushion work? What nobility (or the opposite) does it impart to the music? What serenity (or the opposite)? What zest for life (or the opposite)? The interesting thing is that the pipes are telling us, during every moment the organ is playing, about this wind matrix they draw their unity from; yet we tend not to notice, and indeed, we are forever praising or blaming the pipes, action, case, placement, acoustics for properties of the organ which derive mainly from the character of the wind matrix. We see this matrix through a veil, darkly. We will never see it clearly. But we can at least recognize its existence and pay it some measure of the respect it is owed.

In Memory of Carl Theodore Young

[Eulogy given at St. Mary's Church, Rockport, Massachusetts
October 15, 1977]

[Editor's note: Carl Theodore "Ted" Young was a Swedish-American cabinetmaker who came to work for the Fisk firm during his retirement years—simply because he loved woodworking and couldn't stand being idle. As Charles Fisk's eulogy implies, he found his way into the hearts of all his fellow employees, and earned the respect of all both for his consummate skill in woodworking and his unassuming personality. Although born on Cape Ann, he had a great desire to visit the land of his forebears. This desire was finally realized in 1977, when, despite some risk to an already-weakened heart, he embarked on a tour of Scandinavia with a group of fellow Scandinavian-Americans. Just a day or two before the group was to return, Ted died of a heart attack in a Copenhagen hotel—but he had seen Sweden at last.]

Carl Theodore Young.
Ted Young.

Generous with his talents.
Generous with his skills.
Generous with his energy.

Whose fine craftsmanship was but an outward expression of the inner man.

Ted Young began work at the Skinner Organ Company in Dorchester *four years* before I was born. I first met him one day almost a decade ago, when he came into our organ workshop, looked us over and said that he would be retiring from his job shortly, and after that he'd "just as soon" work with us. . . . I recall being somewhat curiously unimpressed with him at the time—yes of course, his pedigree of accomplishment was long and persuasive: ten years in the organ business for three organ builders (all of them now defunct), spent the war years in the shipyard, worked on rich men's yachts at Lawley's boat yard, *built houses in his spare time*—but I wondered, "Can this big, open faced man with the flat, broad, just-south-of-Boston accent make the necessary adjustment, the necessary *conversion* of mind to become one of *us*? Can he adapt to anything as *off beat* as what we are doing?" Little did I know that it was *we* who would be readjusting and converting ourselves to him—not he to us.

I'd like to say a few words here about craftsmanship, because it seems to mean so much to the young these days. There is a great tendency to think that fine craftsmanship implies infinite care with all details—as if when you are at work you must execute every maneuver to perfection because somebody up high—our Creator, perhaps—is watching your every move. The trouble with this notion of craftsmanship is that it's totally impractical. Nobody can afford to pay you while you take the time to make all your infinitesimals perfect unless you are willing to work today for the thirty cents an hour Ted got when he first went to work at Skinner's in 1921.

Ted, more than anyone else, taught us the true answer to this burning question: that craftsmanship is the art of making things *quickly* and *with just the right amount of attention to detail*, no more, no less. Good craftsmanship, as he showed us, is work that leaves the workman's hands quickly, is not lovingly handled—and fondled. Work never lingered in Ted's hands. Working just half a day, Ted Young could accomplish as much as anyone else in the shop could in a full day. Of course, he was an immensely vigorous and efficient man, even in the years we knew him. Goodness knows what he must have been like—as I'm sure many of you could tell us—before his first heart attack cut him down to the size, more or less, of the rest of us mortals.

It was a sublime symbiosis that we shared with Ted these last few years. For his part, he loved the workshop and what the workshop produced, and I venture to say that the workshop kept him alive, in the way that it spiritually nourishes all of us who work within it. But we and the workshop received from Ted far more than he ever received from us. Not only did he give us *all* of his energy, he gave us a light to steer by. All the wisdom of the century before seemed to stir within him, and to blaze itself forth—not in his words to be sure, for his words were the barest clues to what he was really thinking—but in his actions. He was Father to all of us collectively, and then to each one of us individually, each in a different way. For the youngest of us he stood—and *will* stand, always—for the old-fashioned virtues: good work, a clear conscience, the well-rooted life of former times, superb teacher-by-example, superb Father—without the generation-gap, superb friend. For the middle-aged among us he was all those things too, but most of all a marvel in human form, and most marvellous perhaps, because he seemed to know so well *who he was, and why he was here*. This means so much to people who do not yet have those answers.

I cannot say that he also seemed to know where he was going. Death and the idea of departing from us seemed to trouble Ted at least as much as anything in his life; one sensed that he felt it close upon him, and one wished so many times for ways in which to reassure him that everything was going to be all right, even after Death. I feel confident that he has found that out now, finally—something for which we here should all be very, very grateful. Somehow we can all sense now that Ted is O.K.

Nothing, after all, is wasted. A life with so much in it that was perfect has touched the lives of each one of us here today and has left behind it far, far more than the usual evidences of love. Though this life is gone, it will go on touching us as long as we can remember it—and how can we ever forget? But it was best said for us in a poem of Robert Burns:

"Take him for a' and a', he was a man.
We *will not live* to see his like again."

Singular Aspects
of the Organ Reform in America

[Notes for an unpublished article or talk, written ca. 1980]

> "It will generally be found, I think, that the more a man appreciates and admires the soul of another people the less he will attempt to imitate it; he will be conscious that there is something in it too deep and too unmanageable to imitate. The Englishman who has a fancy for France will try to be French; the Englishman who admires France will be obstinately English."
>
> G. K. CHESTERTON, "French and English," an essay

CHESTERTON'S OBSERVATION is probably still correct for most of European culture. One still expects a well-established Parisian to be primarily concerned with Parisian culture; though interested in foreign ways, he is by no means ready to think or live according to the ideas that prevail in, say, the city of Hamburg. Meanwhile the modern Hamburger feels much the same about Paris. And these feelings reach into the past: A German musician of today may become an expert on the 18th-century delicacies of Jean Philipe Rameau, but his countrymen will cease to listen if during the process of becoming he loses his objectivity.

In America, a different attitude has held sway for many, many years. Educated Americans, supposing themselves to be culturally inferior to their European counterparts, and being at no pains to conceal this supposed inferiority, have borrowed from European sources wherever possible. Nowhere in American culture has this borrowing been more of a habit than in the domain of serious music, and especially in the domain of serious church music.

American culture has always been eclectic, profiting from the knowledge, skills and inspiration that newcomers brought from abroad. Once established on these shores, an immigrating artist or craftsman was likely to experience a release from the constraints of orthodox practices of his native land. With an ingenuity that would have been unwelcome elsewhere, he felt impelled to weave together strands from many disparate sources. Sometimes the result was an entirely new creation.

This has happened at least twice in the history of American organ building.

Church music in the 19th-century American city was dominated by English-taught musicians, and thus it was only natural that American organs should imitate English models in form and spirit throughout the 19th century. From 1900 to 1930 they fell under the spell of an imported Englishman, Robert

Hope-Jones. He was the mechanical genius who, in the name of serious music, unwittingly devised the first truly American organ—the Cinema Organ.

About 1930, when talking pictures had silenced the Cinema Organ, another Englishman, G. Donald Harrison, arrived in America to devise a new kind of organ for serious music. He called it the American Classic Organ. This was an American response to the Franco-German Organ Reform Movement, whose main concern was the revival of the so-called Bach organ. Once settled in America Harrison became greatly affected by the fresh research on German and French organ building practices in the Baroque. His grand endeavor was to synthesize all known styles of organ building into a single instrument capable of playing all varieties of serious organ music. We now know so much more about early organ building practices that Harrison's attempt seems naive. Yet, as so often happens with inspired efforts that succeed despite—or perhaps because of—a certain amount of misinformation, his results were artistic. Indeed, the American Classic Organ as conceived by G. Donald Harrison during the late thirties still commands our respect, even though it falters in its original purpose of imparting authenticity to performances of serious organ music.

America is a land of problem-solvers, of tinkerers, of people who are given to making adjustments to the culture they borrow from abroad. Hope-Jones and Harrison came to America partly because it offered them the chance to do things differently, to apply the established rules in new ways. And the result of recombining the old ideas is usually practical and interesting, and is sometimes quite beautiful.

To capture beauty while reaching towards the illusive ideal: that is one version of the American dream—perhaps the only viable version left in today's world. In his organs Harrison achieved beauty, and American organ builders are going right on with his dream, his quest for the all-purpose organ, knowing that such a thing may not really exist, but that results of great beauty are possible along the path.

In Europe, large sums of government money have supported a throng of organ builders during the past thirty years, especially in Germany, but the bureaucracies have made serious mistakes in advising and controlling organ builders. Where the quest for the "Classic" or all-purpose organ is pursued, it is generally within the context of strong national traditions that limit the scope of the product.

More often, European thinking now takes the position that it is useless to try to produce a single organ for all varieties of music. If you wish to hear French organ music of a certain style and period, you must hear it on a French organ of the same style and period, or else on a modern copy of such an organ. This argument disregards certain inherent difficulties. Most of the antique organs of Europe are so infirm or so mutilated that their original builders would disown them if they could hear them; on the other hand, existing modern copies suffer from the loss of "heart" and interest that the act of mere copying engenders. Moreover, and more importantly, most congregations can afford only one organ, but would never be content with music from just one locale and era.

The solution seems to be to retain much, but not all, of Harrison's elusive ideal while trying for results that are no less beautiful. Knowing that an all-purpose organ *cannot* exist, we can still strive for excellence in a *multi-purpose* organ. Setting our sights at this more practical level, we would hope to discover new ways of solving old problems; we would hope to see new ways of combining modern technology with old-time craftsmanship. Keeping in mind that each new organ is always different from every other, even in those few instances when the setting alone makes the difference, we would hope always to create an object of both visual and aural beauty. There is reason to think that our American heritage will help us in this endeavor.

A CHARLES FISK MISCELLANY

Greensboro College Organ and Church Music Conference, 1980

[Editor's note: What follows is taken from a transcript of a recording made during a discussion entitled "Historic French Organs and Modern Organ Building" chaired by Charles Fisk and Fenner Douglass. Inevitably, much of the discussion had to do with historical and technical facts. The excerpts quoted below were chosen because of what they reveal of Charles Fisk's insights and opinions.]

[In response to questions concerning manual organ blowing:]

I WILL MAKE one very interesting remark which is for the organ builders here. And that is, the other day I went with George Taylor to see the Tannenberg organ in Madison [Virginia]. The Tannenberg organ has exactly this; it still has its original blowing equipment. It is one of the few organs in America—old ones—that is still blown in the eighteenth-century way. And the very interesting thing is . . . we found that when the [electric] blower would simply have one bellows full of air and the other not, this blew the organ all right, but the wind was less stable in that situation than if both bellows were inflated. Now, if you think about that a minute, what this means is that if both bellows have air in them, one is going to be giving air usually when the other is not giving air, even though both are ready to give air. There is some phenomenon that I don't quite understand which means that if you fill both bellows and let them both go, always one will seem to go and then the other, if you see what I mean. Now it seems to be that . . . if you've got both bellows full . . . and one of them is delivering the air to the organ, if there are pulses coming back and forth . . . in the wind line, in other words, if the air is sloshing back and forth in the wind line, which is what happens when the wind is unsteady, the bellows which is not delivering air apparently will give a little pulse of air into the system, like a winker, whenever the pressure goes down below a certain point, and this acts as a stabilizing influence and it might be one reason why the French often used to use three bellows instead of two—even when one man was blowing the organ. There is some stabilization that occurs there, and what this means to us, of course, is that these wind supplies we've been building which have a blower and a single bellows of this kind, perhaps they're not quite as stable as some of the old ones—which I'm very sorry to report.

You see, organ blowing is an art. If you don't believe it, go and try one of these one-manual organs with a foot-thing, and you will discover that you have great difficulty in sort of letting go of the pedal at the bottom of its stroke so that you don't get a hiccup in the wind when you do that. In other words, if I'm going to blow this organ [in a diagram drawn on a blackboard] by hand by pulling these ropes, I am going to have to initiate the upward motion of this very gently so as not to go sort of sucking this [check] valve shut. The valve will be open letting the last remains of air out of this bellows into the trunk, and I will then lift this up in such a way as not to slam the door shut and shake the wind. But, if I am not careful, I will shake the wind. Then, I get up to the top, I'm now ready to let go. Just imagine what happens if I just go *yuck* like that and let go. This weight and the whole top of the bellows comes down and goes *nyaah*, just like that. And you know . . . I am sure that if you didn't like the organist, you could make life miserable. . . .

But, if you believe, as I do, that the more like an animate object the organ can be made, the better it is. If you believe that, then there is something to the notion that here is some imperfect guy, maybe trying to be perfect, but he isn't quite, who is out in back blowing the organ and . . . every now and then as you are playing you hear this thing as if the organ, you know, sort of shifted itself in its chair or something like that—I mean, something that makes you think that it is not just a machine.

[In response to a question concerning pipe metal:]

One good thing about tin pipework is that, ideally, tin pipework is quite thin-walled. There is not much point to making tin pipework with thick walls, because one of the reasons for the tin is to get some of the character of the tin's vibration into the sound. And Silbermann, especially, used tin pipework that was just terribly thin. You hardly could see how you could develop a decent tone with pipe walls that thin, and yet it comes out beautifully. But it is almost an ephemeral sound; there's no heaviness to it at all. . . . You know, if you would take an organ like this and build it out of lead pipework, it would just have a terrible heaviness; formidable sound. As it is, it sort of glazes—I mean, when you get it going . . . it has a foundation to it, but there's a certain clatter going on up above it all which keeps you from thinking that things are really fundamental. And, in fact, I would say generally that the European organs, even the ones with what we would call "bad specifications," probably almost never had the foundational quality that we've heard from organs of the twenties and so forth in this country. I just don't think that the Continent produced those. But I've seen a few German organs of the Romantic period, and yes, they've got loads of eight foot stops, but you would be surprised how gentle a lot of that stuff is; no single voice is really blustering at you the way you find in—oh, anything that's following the time of Hope-Jones.

[In response to comments on historical accuracy in playing:]

Well, we're afflicted with a love for antiques. And I don't know what to think about it; all I know is that we are. We—essentially we know too much. We know too much literature, on the one hand, and then the organist's great failing I feel is—the serious organist who isn't just having a good time around the theater organ or something like that (which I think is a fine thing to do, by the way)—the serious organist finds himself paying too much attention to the notes, and deifying the notes on the page. I mean the notes on the page weren't anything that meant much to those [French Romantic] guys. I mean, none of us can hear Lemmens, but I'll bet that he played games with some of those [Bach] pieces.

I don't think that many of us who are related to the organ will deny that if there is a god of music it ought to be Bach. The trouble with having a god is that you've got to deify him; you've got to bow down before him, and this is a problem. My friend . . . Melville Smith used to play beautifully almost everything except Bach. And I would try to get him to play Bach and it would come out sort of stilted and square which was far from Mel's nature. And he would say, "You don't like the way I play that piece, do you?" And . . . there wasn't any way to say that that wasn't true, because it wasn't up to his standard. But he would just sort of put Bach aside because, of course, the thing he felt so much for was this old . . . he loved the French music of all periods, but Bach put him off, you see. And I think probably Bach plus Lemmens was putting off a lot of people, especially Lefébure-Wély, just about the time we are talking about. Here comes—the Gospel is sort of dribbling in under our feet here—what are we going to do about it? You know, I think there must have been some of that involved because . . . there is a tendency to get very serious when you are talking about Bach, and you don't have to be serious when you are talking about Lefébure-Wély, and all of those guys just before the Revolution I guess were—mostly had their tongues in their cheeks. I don't know. It's the way it sounds anyway.

Well, it's been characteristic of our time for—first of all—for there to be such a thing as "good music," unquote. And then you have to decide what "good music" is. It includes Bach; it includes Schütz, we have discovered; it's maybe starting to include Scheidemann. You know, you go looking around through the libraries and you keep finding this stuff and somebody who is really smart will say, "I just know that that's a good piece; I don't know how I'm going to show it, but I just know that it is." Then eventually somebody does show that it's a good piece, and then you are stuck with it; stuck with it in the sense that you really feel as though you have an obligation to try to make that piece sound the way it ought to sound. And this is our problem. It's not a problem that came much before our time.

[Concerning flue pipe voicing:]

 . . . one of the standard thoughts in America has been that you should never cut up principal pipes higher than one quarter. These days—in our own work in our workshop—we almost never use a quarter cutup. For mixture work the standard cutup is one third. . . . But what the cutup does is to determine the ratio of energy that goes into overtones versus energy that goes into fundamental. With a low cutup you get more overtones; with a high cutup you get more fundamental.

 . . . But the French plein jeu was just not apparently blown as hard as the German plein jeu. And Dom Bedos, in fact, shows us low cutups in his book. And you go into even that Cavaillé-Coll at Epernay and you find quarter cutups or sometimes lower, I think. Now this means that you take the fulness out of the sound.

 . . . one of the biggest problems has been that [organ builders] in this country . . . probably still do think that you can't have a cutup higher than a quarter. And the result has been, in my opinion, instruments that have only a top and no middle. There is nothing rounded about the sound that you make in this way.

 . . . it's from the French, not from copying the Germans. That's my point.

Look at Poitiers. You will find very low cutups in the plein jeu. And it's French; because the French were not depending on the plein jeu to do the all-out thing. In other words, the French relied on these reeds—this is classic French—and Cavaillé-Coll too, for heaven's sake—the French had this big battery of armaments in the form of their reeds which the Germans couldn't stand. And therefore they could let themselves have—especially in reverberant churches—a glittering plein jeu which sounded very full and so forth, but it could probably put out twice as much sound as it was putting out. Whereas the

Germans depended, for filling the church, on blowing every pipe to its maximum. And in order to do this they had to have high cutups. And they did have high cutups. But this was unknown or unavailable to the people of the American Orgelbewegung.

[Concerning eclecticism and the creative process:]

We're in trouble every inch of the way, largely because, as I said before, we know too much. If we could go back to being as naive as we were twenty years ago, that would be very nice. We could still think that we could solve all these problems in one organ. I think it's true that you can't really solve all these problems in one organ. I think what you can do with one organ is to make it very good for something, and by making it very good for something and then by doctoring it here and there, you can make it so that it is quite passable for an awful lot else. But I don't think that it is possible to create an instrument that's perfect for everything. I would never say that.

I can only tell you how I go—I mean, more or less how I go about thinking about these things. First of all, I don't think about anybody else but myself. I am apt to get various pieces of music on my mind and carry it around on what I call my Muzak; we all have Muzak up here—I'm sure that bothers us sometimes; other times it is pleasant to listen to. But I just sit around thinking, "what would be nice?" and "what would work?" And, now for example, at House of Hope, the Stellwagen Brustwerk would never have been there if, before that organ was really finished and designed, I hadn't gone, thanks to Wellesley College, to Europe and seen what Stellwagen did at Jakobi, Lübeck, the small organ. . . . And it just seems to me that anything that was as good as that thing in Lübeck, you just couldn't hate it no matter what organ it went into, unless it took the place of something that was desperately needed. And I think I was right.

. . . The things that I do, I feel almost as though they're nothing that I control, really. It has to do with what occurs to me and to other people that would be nice to do. That's really what it is.

I'd like to say something else, though, and that is that I think that if an eclectic organ has an excuse for working, one reason is that it avoids a number of misconceptions about organs—about old organ building—that are very prevalent. I've already mentioned the business of the cutup. There is a whole directory full of mistakes that I feel people are making these days based on misunderstanding of what was actually done at any time. And, in other words, if our organ builders today really understood what it is that makes a Cavaillé-Coll organ beautiful, or then, on the other hand, the same builder really understood what it was that made a Clicquot beautiful, or what made a Schnitger beautiful, they would be able to leave out a tremendous body of misinformation which stands in the way of good organ building today. This whole business of studying old organs and so forth, you see, it's a wonderful thing; but be awfully careful how you interpret it when you are looking at an old organ. When you see and hear things, be careful about how you decide that Schnitger made something beautiful. Or that you're very careful to decide what it is about such and such a flute at Steinkirchen which is beautiful. There are certain things . . . and I guess I am talking more about voicing than anything— there are certain things that go into voicing—into good voicing—that were really followed by all of these people together . . . Cavaillé-Coll wouldn't have succeeded if he hadn't somehow detected the essence of the thing that is beautiful in Clicquot and the other people that he must have learned from, and whose organs he learned from. The trouble is that we have people who will make things with low cutups and open toe holes just because they are told that is good. And that is what we cannot do. And if everybody—as I've said in print—if everybody would simply use his own ears and ask himself what he thinks is beautiful, and not listen to what people tell him is beautiful, we would be an awful lot better off.

[Cavaillé-Coll] grew up with the sound of old organs in his ears; he had to. There weren't any Cavaillé-Coll organs when he was growing up—I mean, none of his. And the idea, you see, that the idea of perfection comes from listening to things that aren't perfect. I mean . . . every organ pipe, no matter how humble and awful, still has the germ of something that is a beautiful idea within it; it's very funny. And I think that Cavaillé-Coll would have heard in—you know, walking around in the churches as he was—he would have heard things that just swept him off his feet coming out of who knows whose organs . . . I mean, you don't know where that was, you don't know where that experience occurred to him. But there would have been situations—and don't forget they were so much luckier in having these churches that would take a sound which wasn't what we'd call distinguished, and somehow emphasize this beautiful quality that exists no matter how humble the pipe. And really, organ building is a question of distillation, just as composition is. I mean composition—good composition—is a question of taking ideas that have come into your mind all this time (surely this is it) and somehow peeling away the part of it which isn't quite germane to what you want to do, and getting right at the thing that somehow gels together as the beautiful idea in your mind, or the thing that really interests you—the thing that you really suddenly feel that you wanted—you could have done.

[In response to questions on electricity and registrational aids:]

I think that one answer would be that we haven't solved the question of how to move the sliders except by hand. You can make all kinds of things that aren't sliders. I mean, heck, you could build a spring chest if you could figure out how to work the springs—the little valves that are all held up by springs.

But I think we haven't solved the question of how you run the sliders. And myself, I mean—make something that will last, and something that doesn't give more trouble by far than the old tried and true method. You see, if you build a mechanical stop action, you are building something which should last as long as the rest of the organ. The instant you put an electric motor in, for example, to drive the sliders, this seems as if it should be perfectly all right until you recognize that almost no electric motor is asked to run more than maybe thirty or forty years, and you are hoping to have the organ run much longer than that. The instant you build something into an organ which you know will have to be replaced within a much shorter time than the rest of the organ, you know you are building in the possibility of its being disposed of at the time that goes bad. Because, if an organ is giving trouble, as we all know, the people who have the control of the decision of whether to replace it or not don't understand why it has to be replaced; I mean all they know is that it doesn't work. And so it is very easy to replace an organ when some part of it goes really bad, and if it develops electric motor trouble in forty years, what do you then do? You ... can't buy those motors; nobody is going to be making them. And somebody will say, well there will be something else that is better. Well, I doubt it. I think a large part of the mechanical stop action idea is retreat from something which doesn't seem to be—you know, a wise thing to build on. There is, of course, the other problem, that there are very few ... non-mechanical stop actions ... even in a pitman organ action, in which the act of getting the stop on is as precise as it is by pulling a knob on a slider chest. In other words, if I want a particular stop to come on at a particular time—if I really want it to come on really at just that moment, I know I can do it by pulling the knob on an old fashioned tracker organ. But even in a pitman chest I don't have that feeling—even though the response of the stop action is very quick—there is something off-putting about this little knob that I am just moving a little bit to get the thing to happen. It is really the same thing that has to do with playing the keys in a much more clumsy situation. And I think that it is possible to argue that mechanical stop action is more musical than electric stop action. I really think it is. But then you have to say that it isn't more musical if the performer is trying to make a whole lot of stop changes all by himself and gets into trouble doing it—and that's quite a normal thing.

[Concerning the meantone organ at Wellesley College:]

I think... that this whole organ is, in a way, an educational toy. I mean, it isn't a toy, but it sure is educational. Any organ with fourteen keys per octave is going to be educational to people used to only twelve. The whole object of the Wellesley organ, of course, is to show everyone, including me, a lot of things that we won't be able to find out any other way. I've not had the privilege of being around an organ of any size which was tuned in meantone; or at least I haven't been around one for very long that was tuned in meantone.... The addition of two keys per octave makes it so that you can play in two more keys safely than in just the ones that are available in meantone. And the reason we are building an organ like this is because there were examples of these in existence before the Thirty Years War in Germany. In fact, the organ that Heinrich Schütz had in Dresden is described by Praetorius, and he gives exactly the layout of the keyboards; of how the keys are situated and with what notes they represent. And it's according to this information that we are building the organ—and other information, of course, comes from observing organs.

And... I suspect that when the organ is done, a lot of people will say, "Why bother?" I think the answer to the question, "Why bother?" will only... emerge gradually. And it's very possible that some of the answers that come out of it will just make everybody very unhappy anyway, because they will realize that some of these pieces they've been playing and thinking they were hearing, they hadn't really heard—just because of a simple thing like tuning. I mean it's only within the last—what, ten years, that we've gotten away from everybody being in equal temperament. And it may be that, you know, equal temperament is something that we should cleave to. I don't know the answer to that question. But I feel that part of what we are about here as organists—and certainly in schools—is, as long as our forefathers have somehow instilled in us the desire to learn all this stuff about people that are all dead, then, we've got to go ahead with it until somebody says, "Come on, stop; you can't go on and do this any more."

[Some final thoughts on copying old organs and eclecticism:]

[To Fenner Douglass:] I think really, you and I... agree that—you talk about organs which are not true (I mean I've heard you for years) and the thing that worries you is organs (if I may be so bold)—is organs which don't cleave to any particular idea of what an organ is—that are just reaching out in all directions at once. And I think when I say that people who build organs are laboring under illusions of what was really done in any really classical or romantic time in the way of good organ building, I think really those are saying the same thing.

I will probably never really give up the idea of trying to—you know, add a little wing on here that will produce something else that I like; I am that American.... we won't do this to the Wellesley organ, but... I don't think we'll ever—I will ever—get out of the habit of thinking, "My, wouldn't it be nice if...." I'd say, "Fenner won't like this, but wouldn't it...."

I would just like to say that I feel sorry for us—I don't mean you and me, I mean everybody in the room—because we are hawking after something that is awfully difficult to achieve. And we wouldn't do it if we didn't have an idea that by doing what we are doing—whether it's playing or building—that we would turn some corner and there would be something more beautiful, more pleasure to us than has come along.... I think that it would be much more fun to have been a Cavaillé-Coll, who could just go ahead and do his thing, running rough-shod over everything that was in his way and not having a guilty conscience about it. I bet he never had a moment's worry about what he had busted.

But there is something about our age that makes us the way we are, and I don't know what it is. It has to do with the fact that we are never really sure of anything.

... copying, as I've said to you before, is impossible.

If you create something that's your own during copying, that's fun. But if all you are doing is copying, it will never work.

[Wellesley again:] ... there is so little to go on. I mean there are no organs from the time except for the Compenius organ at Hillerød in Denmark, which was a very unusual instrument. And I think this leaves great gaps in our knowledge about what to do. And again, I simply have the feeling that we will have to fill those gaps with trying to feel the way it felt to be one of those people. If you could manage to feel the way it felt to be a Compenius, or a Fritzsche, in those times, while you were doing work just like theirs, that would be quite something, and perhaps that's the great difficulty. It's so difficult to—I mean, it's hard enough to feel like your father felt. The world has surrounded him with differences.... The whole world just felt like a different place. To put yourself in his shoes and get to be him or that sort of thing is very difficult indeed. And you know, it's like being an actor, almost. You've got to turn yourself into this person if you are going to do a convincing performance. And that's not easy.

Excerpts from Letters

[Editor's note: The following excerpts are drawn from miscellaneous correspondence. They cover a wide range of subject matter, from personal reminiscences to aesthetic ideas to commentary on various instruments.]

As you may surmise, the building of tracker action is a matter of great interest to us. We have studied it at considerable length, from the literature, from modern European instruments and through our own several restorations of tracker organs, in anticipation of the day when we expect to be building more tracker organs than any other kind.

Charles Fisk to Hubert Lamb, January 31, 1956

"Are you familiar with the First Unitarian Church in Newburyport? It is a *very* fine old church, built in 1801, with a steeple which, it is whispered, may have been designed by Christopher Wren; Whoever designed it and the rest of the church knew exactly what he was about in any case. There is a certain appropriate nautical influence which I have not seen in any other New England church. It is big scale, as we say in the organ business, and the acoustics are pretty good.

We have decided that, although we could do a better electrification job than others, we will not take the job unless we can do it our way.... But as things stand, the chance of getting the job under our self-imposed restrictions are very small; they do not want tracker manuals, and we do not wish to waste our time, which is becoming increasingly valuable, doing a third rate job which it would hurt us to do, inwardly, I mean. And as you know, the electrification of a tracker organ is never really successful; the action is always slower than a new electro-pneumatic, the unsteadiness of the wind, rather attractive in some tracker organs, becomes a fault, and the organ becomes just plain dull.

So what we need, or rather, what the organ needs, is the incidence of more crazy men upon the scene.... We are proposing this more for the good of the organ than anything else; we don't care too much about the job, but a church like this one *should* have an organ in its original condition, not just a half-baked made-over mess.

... I suppose that, as an organ builder, I should develop Holtkamp's steely indifference to the old. After all, it is not mine, not an expression of my feeling and thought. I would not build an organ this way, even if allowed to. But I cannot help but feel that preservation of the old has a place along with creation of the new. Am I wrong? Who can say.

Charles Fisk to Melville Smith, February 16, 1956

At its best, an organ is more than just something somebody thought of adding after the church was finished. Instead, the organ should be an important part of the architecture of the church. People should be able to look at the organ and, without hearing it, know that here resides the musical soul of the church. Such is always the case in the old churches of Europe where the organ nearly always adorns the west wall.... In these churches the sound does not emanate from some hole leading out to the eaves or up to the attic....

I fear that I cannot and must not try to lecture on the aesthetique of the organ in this letter, but your people obviously need to have their imaginations caught by the vision of what an organ can and should but seldom does mean to a church. We suffer a great deal from a lack of good examples. Most organs and most churches are dull and disorderly, so that it is no wonder that people can see no farther than an electronic organ or a new dishwasher for the kitchen.

Charles Fisk to Peter M. Hewitt, February 16, 1957

[Concerning a young man interested in organ building] It is important, first, for anyone to understand that there *isn't* any future in the organ business, in the usual sense. A love of organs can be compared to any other handicap, physical or mental: it is only a question of how to get along in spite of it. I think you understand that I myself have never once regretted quitting physics for my present pursuit, but a certain blindness to common sense is characteristic of my particular affliction! Seriously, if your young friend would like to talk with me, I would be pleased to oblige, and some good might conceivably come of it. I trust he is about to enter college at just this turning, which he ought to do even if he intends to be a ditch digger.

... In my book, occupation is the most highly illumined leaf of all; I suffer for those who are not able to follow the occupation of their choice.

Charles Fisk to Richard H. Van Kleeck, August 29, 1961

When I think of you, it is most especially of the time we sang together in the Mahler Second with the San Francisco Symphony—a rather wonderful experience, all in all. I have always warmed to the idea that despite our dedication to instruments which flourished in earlier times—organs and bells, that is—we neither of us would deny the persuasiveness of a late, late romantic symphony. That is certainly as it should be.

Yes of course, tracker organs. Since about two years ago I have resolved to build no more electric action at all, and I think the demand for mechanical action is such that we shall be kept up to our ears in work despite the resolution. I hope you will someday be able to hear the Baltimore organ. It is a serious effort to build an organ in the classical style, no holds barred, and it has come off very well. With such an organ one can see so plainly why certain things were done as they were in the old days. Although this organ is very strict, I do not fancy that strictness in all things is essential to a good instrument. This organ has no Swell, but I think that a Swell is not necessarily an evil and most of our instruments have them. Also electrically controlled stop action. Also combinations. Many of the later and lately-beloved effects are possible on a good instrument; the essence of it is this: that the pipes must be of the kind which are sensitive to the *way* in which they are winded, and, correspondingly, the method of winding has to be controllable by the player. Upon these two rules hang all the law and the prophets.

        Charles Fisk to Ronald Barnes, December 13, 1961

[To a distant relative] Yes of course, I also remember the fascination of that reed organ in the wash house; I can recall the setting perfectly. I remember being surrounded by the other children, they playing with various things, occasionally the organ, with which I, however, was undivertibly enthralled. Later on, my mother bought me (for ten dollars) a similar organ, to which I much later added a pedalboard in order to be able to play some of the great organ repertoire which my growing interest had brought me to know. Still later I set aside my intentions in the field of Physics to learn organ building, and today I have my own modest establishment, which, however small, affords me the greatest pleasure.

 One can little guess what slight exposure will project him into his life's work. By the very fact that I recall that day at the Nobles' so clearly, I can only suppose it was a day of the greatest import in forming and directing me. I was ten, which means that it was twenty-seven years ago this summer.

        Charles Fisk to Ann Noble, March 26, 1962

The news of Melville [Smith's] death has just now reached us here. It comes as a frightful shock; this despite the feeling I have had this year that Melville might not be with us much longer. I feel very low in my mind.

 We won't be able to replace Melville, Hubert, because he is irreplaceable. That particular perception and love for his favorite musical style, the 17th century French, was unique with him, insofar as my ears have ever told me. His particular way with the keyboard was his alone. I never knew anyone who handled the keyboard the way he did, and for me it was not perhaps the only way, but the best way.

 The last several times I saw Melville I asked him please, for our sakes, to put as many things on tape as he could. I also asked him whether he had any really good students who were catching on to his way. . . . Perhaps Frank Taylor is the only one who, by association, has really picked up some sizeable portion of the essence of Melville's way. Melville did not by his personality impress people as being an authority on anything, and this is too bad; it means that he has passed from among us without leaving what he might have left, or what we should have gleaned from him.

Charles Fisk to Hubert Lamb, July 16, 1962

Thanks for your kind words about Westerly. In a way it is a Holtkamp Organ, perhaps because it reflects an attitude acquired in Cleveland—an attitude which always was, and still is, the basis for distinction between American and European instruments.

Charles Fisk to Walter Holtkamp, Jr., April 18, 1966

Were you to come to work here, in due course you could learn all that an organ builder needs to know. There are better regulated establishments than ours in which everything is 'down pat,' and in which the techniques of organ building are perhaps more clearly set forth. For some reason the organs we build are superior to organs built by these well-regulated establishments; I am not sure why this is so, but I think it has to do with the fact that everyone here has to do much of his own thinking and planning, once he has learned the rudiments.

Charles Fisk to David M. Eakin, March 19, 1968

Margaret, if you visited churches in Spain you perhaps noticed the singular feature of Spanish organs which is the profusion of Trumpet pipes projecting horizontally from just below the front pipes. In the rest of the world these are known as Spanish Trumpets, or Trompettes-en-Chamade, and this ancient way of placing the Trumpet pipes is now becoming fairly popular. We have even done it in two of our organs. I am sure the visual intent (not exactly Christian) is to connote naval artillery—the Spanish obviously wanted their organs to look like galleons. Perhaps it is a good thing we didn't put Spanish Trumpets in the organ at Zion church [in Souderton, Pennsylvania], which indeed looks like a sailboat, but an unarmed one!

Charles Fisk to Mr. & Mrs. Lake Clemmer, August 30, 1968

Last fall I cranked out a "baroque" [trumpet] mouthpiece on our little lathe (from another mouthpiece, of course). It was not especially good, but it pointed up some thoughts which I have had milling around in my mind, ideas which you probably are well aware of, but I'll mention them anyway:

The sharp corner at the throat in the old mouthpieces seems to have the effect of decoupling the activity in the mouthpiece from the bore. Thus you can start a note in the decoupled mouthpiece without having much interference from the bore. Just the opposite of the traditional French horn where the coupling is very, very strong and the bore forces the characteristic 'bubble' on the attack. The bore 'kicks back' immediately in the case of the French horn, and the tone does not stabilize quickly; the attack is prolonged.

I see the modern trumpet mouthpiece with its conical (soft cornered) throat as an effort to make the half-length instrument sound something like the original full-length instrument. Thus, you have only half the length of tubing, but if you couple it closely to the mouthpiece, then the bore will 'kick back' more and will slow down the attack a bit, making it more like that of the old trumpet, where there was twice the air column to set into motion.

After all, the fastest-speaking lip vibrated aerophon would be the mouthpiece without *any* horn attached. Quick alright, but without the sense of weight in the attack that comes with the long tube.

Value judgement: I feel that in all the old symphonies, through Beethoven, where the brass consists only of trumpets and horns, it is insane to use anything but the old form of trumpet. It isn't that the tone is so wrong, but rather that the attack is wrong. If the trumpets are half-length they speak (i.e., stabilize on their note) twice as rapidly as the full-length trumpet would. This is especially bad because even the old trumpets were always half the length of the horns; the new trumpets are *one-quarter* the length of the horns, and have pecked out their note long before the horns have stabilized, so that unanimity of the brass speech is lost. Of course this is not so true if the horn players have ruined the essence of their instrument by using trumpet-like mouthpieces and the short B flat upper end of the double horn.

Nobody seems to reflect that those stupid dominant-tonic brass parts in the works of Mozart and Haydn can add nobility only if they come from a goodly length of plumbing. If they come out of a modern D trumpet they add nothing that couldn't be obtained from a well trained mouton.

I think Bate and the others are right in thinking that the hard-cornered throat produces edge tones like an organ pipe, and perhaps even chiff. If you use a hard-cornered mouthpiece in a half-length trumpet, you get a breathy quality which has to be the air jet splitting on the sharp edge of the throat. And of course that breathy quality will always begin practically immediately, long before the note has stabilized. This is the essence of chiff in an organ pipe, i.e., a noise, harmonic or not, which comes at the very beginning, as if in lieu of "good tone," and which is replaced by the 'good tone' after that has had time to develop.

If the half-length trumpet had evolved before the full-length one, we would be saying that the hard-cornered mouthpiece was an effort to approach in the full-length trumpet the characteristics of the half-length trumpet.

Finally, when all is said and done, the nature of the attack of an instrument is every bit as important as its steady state tone quality, and I think in your exploitations of the earlier trumpets you would do well to emphasize this fact all you can, especially in discussion. Spoken like a true organ builder, eh?

Charles Fisk to Edward Tarr, January 30, 1969

[In response to an inquiry from a college student—now an organ builder—regarding his practices and philosophy]

One of the original reasons, I suppose [for building tracker-action organs], was that I admired Schweitzer and took him at his word with regard to the total scope of the organ reform. There are, of course, all of the musical reasons ordinarily put forth with regard to traditional voicing, slider chests, and mechanical action, which I largely agree with. Certainly I would not now wish to build any other kind of organ, and I suspect that I would say this even if tracker organs were still as unpopular as they were when we began building them.

... Essentially, I believe that we should try to pick up where the classical builders left off and go forward from there—but in the same direction, rather than down the type of blind alley that produced the remotely controlled orchestral organ, or the unit organ. I do not, however, feel that we qualify as antiquarians, for we do too many things differently from the way the old builders did them.

... In a trade as old as organ-building, it is probably impossible to come up with something totally new. Usually we discover that something we think we have "invented" is a modification of an idea a century or two old, or that somebody has simultaneously come up with a nearly identical idea.

"Foreseeing" is not our strongest point. At short range, it looks as if the organ reform and tracker movement are still gaining ground, but it probably won't be much longer before things level off. Because of inflation (which hits crafts such as ours particularly hard) and the seemingly progressive financial worries of churches and colleges, I suspect the "monster" organs will soon become a thing of the past, and that the field for smaller two-manual and even one-manual organs will be expanded. Large firms may tend to shrink a little, and small firms seem to be proliferating at a surprising rate at present—an excellent development, I think.

I would like very much to see some research done into the 20th century roots of the American organ reform as advanced by such personalities as G. Donald Harrison, Walter Holtkamp, Sr., Richard Whitelegg, E. Power Biggs,

Lynnwood Farnam, Ernest White, Carl Weinrich, Melville Smith and other American builders and organists of note who supported and encouraged the movement from around 1930 onward. Perhaps their very closeness to us has led us to overlook the part they played. Many of these people were articulate, writing in the various organ magazines, and as far as I know, nobody has really gone back to find out what they thought. In the beginning, of course, they were only interested in tonal reform. The realization that slider chests and tracker action were part of the "package" came later (although Holtkamp at a very early date recognized the musical value of slider chests).

Charles Fisk to Benjamin G. Mague, March 24, 1970

In preparing yourself for your work as an organ builder . . . the most important thing is to nurture your habits of scholarship after you have left school. Thus, if you later find areas of study in which you are weak, you should be ready to apply the nocturnal approach of the scholar to them. At the same time, it is dreadfully important to leave aside the scholar's approach when it is a question of sawing a board or driving a screw. The proper balance between the head and the hand is very difficult for the craftsman to achieve.

Charles Fisk to Louis Dolive, April 28, 1971

As you know, I have long maintained that the characteristics of the wind supply in an organ are critical, and have indeed written an article about the matter, which has done no more than to make some people think I am off my rocker. All the same, I am not off my rocker, and I look for the day when the subject of wind supply will be pursued in America with seriousness.

Biggsy, recently in East Germany, has lent us half a dozen recordings made on Gottfried Silbermann organs. Heretofore I had never heard anything to speak of in the way of recordings of these instruments, but unless these recordings lie, Silbermann deserves his extraordinary reputation. . . .

On the records, I notice in particular that the wind supplies are unstable, and this in a most unusually musical way—to my ear at least. Especially in the smaller instruments (e.g., Grosshartmannsdorf or Fraureuth) is this my impression.

Charles Fisk to Arthur Howes, July 9, 1971

Your technical remarks about the [Silbermann] pipework are interesting, especially regarding the thin walls of hammered tin and the steep languid faces. We have been experimenting with steep languids for several years now. The chiff is thereby reduced (less nicking is necessary) and the steady state tone is in some ways more highly developed. You *have* to keep the upper lip out; otherwise the windsheet follows the face of the languid upward and "disappears" inside the pipe without making a sound! You have to use higher cutups with the steeper languid face, too.

Charles Fisk to Arthur Howes, November 3, 1971

No doubt tuning is very important with these [historic] organs. We have recently retuned the Harvard Organ in Werckmeister's Second Temperament, and it does indeed make a difference. Actually *all* thirds sound better because this temperament uses only thirds that are narrower or wider than those of equal temperament. The equal temperament third is exactly wrong. It jangles with the just thirds of the tierces, yet is not enough *out* of tune with just thirds to lose that jangling sound and "go off on its own."

More and more I hear people clamoring for a specialized instrument for playing only one segment of the literature. I wonder if this splintering of "The Baroque Organ" into the separate specialized styles is the sign that the Baroque Revival is nearing its end. I'm not sure just how much farther we can go along these lines of perfectionism.

Re cases, we have been using solid wood where we can for some time in the belief that plywood is bad music wood. As to the chief function of the case, I do not know. It does focus the sound and its cavity resonances are very important, but I also think the vibration of the wood is important. Presumably when the wood vibrates, the "Q" of the cavity resonances is much reduced, and this may be good, as cavity resonances discriminate unmercifully against certain pipes inside the case.

Charles Fisk to Arthur Howes, March 16, 1973

The Europeans have more effective ways of training organ builders than we do, and they are more efficient in their organ building methods. The one thing about us that is better, perhaps, is our attitude toward the finished instrument. There is a less impersonal quality in our instruments, and this is a matter of great importance.

Charles Fisk to Takeshi Nakazato, October 26, 1973

We *have* to find a way to keep the windways open. Every decent pipe I looked at [in Europe] had an open windway. The problem is that we have to do it without nicking. Practically every old pipe I saw had a gegenphase [counterface]; many times this showed up only under 10x magnification, but it was there. Cor Edskes thinks the gegenphase was put there by the voicer but I do not—when the voicer does it he creates a burr at the arras between gegenphase and languid which may not be helpful. So I think all pipes should be *made* with a gegenphase. . . .

By the way, don't write off your uncle Gottfried Silbermann. . . . It's interesting to see how he brought the suave French practices over to Saxony and then vitalized them in a German way, mostly by blowing the bjeezus out of everything. In this sense he was gothic.

Charles Fisk to John Brombaugh, May 13, 1974

My only regret about the trip to Groningen is that I could not have made it *years* earlier. When I was 27 and still just learning in the organ business, I could so easily have come to Holland with Ann and somehow managed to work for an organ builder (that was 1952!). But it did not seem easy then and I stayed here instead. I wonder how my ideas about organs would have differed as a result of a long, early experience in Europe. Some day someone will have to make a study of the effect of phonograph records on organ building. I had to learn *so* much from records! And think of Ronald Sharpe in Australia who learned everything he knew from records and a few old 19th-century English organs.

Charles Fisk to Harald Vogel, May 20, 1974

Cabinet resonances: Gak! My impression is that if you erect sticks just defining the *corners* of a cabinet, the Resonance Ghost will take residence immediately. When there is a cabinet resonance, I never try to get rid of it. My only hope is that I can lower the "Q" enough to prevent interference with pipe speech.

I do believe the curved surfaces we have used for roofs over the West Church Great and also the Willimantic/Ipswich/Winchester-Epiphany curves-and-cusps tend to spread the resonance frequencies over a broader band. *Square* boxes, on the other hand, seem worst, i.e., more selective than ordinary *rectangular* boxes. Tilting the roofs, as over the Great flats at Harvard (A. Silbermann always did) also relieves the selectivity, I believe. But the whole business is cut-and-try, as far as I am concerned.

Charles Fisk to George K. Taylor, December 7, 1974

I went to Eddie Flint's memorial concert in Lincoln—quite lovely. John Ferris's choir in truncated form did pieces out of the Concord Anthem Book, which would have been just published when Eddie was Doc Davison's student at Harvard. . . . My own feeling is that some library . . . should start a collection of organ books, beginning with Eddie's library as a nucleus. I don't really need the Dom Bedos. I'll be much better off with Chuck Ferguson's [translated] version together with my Bärenreiter reprint, and I am not one to lay great store by books, as you know. I'm much happier finding out things from people who have read the books.

Charles Fisk to Fenner Douglass, December 1, 1975

I was in East Germany this last spring and saw various Silbermann organs, viz. Rötha, Bad Lausick, Freiberg Dom and Grosshartmannsdorf. The first and last were *excellent* instruments, I felt, and I did my best to understand their workings. You mention the question of the overshot upper lips; this is accomplished not by making the foot small, but rather by making the flat of the foot wider than the body, a bit as though one were to call for quarter mouths for the feet and two-ninths mouths for the bodies. At Grosshartmannsdorf this technique was especially noticeable. Also, his pipes of 2-foot and longer often use the triangular flat for the upper lip which tends to achieve the overshot effect. I regard the overshot lip as one reason for the quality he gets, also the very thin tin walls, the thick languids with uniformly 70° front angles, the use of some nicking, high cutups and, *especially*, the use of open windways in the treble. It is just as I thought, Arthur—you *have* to keep the windways open, even if you must use nicking in order to do it.

I was astonished to see how much like his brother Andreas's work Gottfried's organs *appeared*. If you *look* at either a flue pipe or a reed pipe you might not be able to tell which brother made it. But Gottfried blew everything so much harder than did Andreas, thereby turning the mild and suave French sound into a lusty German sound.

The best of Gottfried Silbermann's work pleases me as much as any work I have ever heard.

Charles Fisk to Arthur Howes, January 21, 1975

As for tuning slides, the reason against using them I suppose is that perhaps they have some effect tonally. I have never known this for sure, but assume it is the case. Also, they can be de-tuned much more easily.

The reasons for using them are, first, the shape of the pipe remains stable once the slides have been adjusted to the pipe tops. This means no smiling pipe mouths, no wrecking of the voicing job by the tuner, no serious problem resetting the pitch or the temperament. Second, if you wish to louden a stop or cut it up after you have tuned it, this is very easy. We find ourselves doing this all the time in finishing an organ, and it is one of the reasons our flue work is well balanced.

So I don't know what the best answer is, but so far this is my choice. It is by no means a popular one with the purists.

Charles Fisk to Gene R. Bedient, June 24, 1975

[In response to some questions from a young organ builder on voicing and scaling]

... we pay very little attention to constant halving ratios.

We have never used open toe holes as a principle. In the trebles of our choruses most pipes have open toe holes, but the rule followed rigorously here is that the windways must be kept open, even if that means some nicking.

Our organs are not copies of anything. Copying in general is a terrible idea, as it stifles original thought. To borrow somebody's scale or cutup or chest design for your own use—that is quite another matter.

The best tonal advice I can give you is to trust your own ears and to be careful about believing what you read or hear said. A good general rule is that the people who do all the talking know the least. The exception to this rule is Dom Bedos. ...

Charles Fisk to Richard Swanson, May 24, 1975

[On concert organ design] The St. Maximin idea of *La Resonance* (Bombarde)—a large division controllable from either the Great or Pedal—would give the possibility of great versatility to any concert organ. Throw in the idea of a Blockwerk which can *also* be played either on the manual or the pedal or both, plus a really able Positive and a full nineteenth century Swell and you may have it.

Charles Fisk to Lawrence Moe, March 1, 1976

You asked for information on the mixtures in the St. Paul organ, and I thought the best way to explain them to you was to send you copies of the actual pipe orders. As you can see, there is nothing very unusual, except that in the Great mixture, I ask for $2/3$ of the pipework to be of hammered lead and $1/3$ to be of hammered $50/50$. The theory is that the lead gives massiveness to the tone, while the tin gives brightness—and both are desirable. In its effect, this mixture is not especially prominent (it blends well with the foundation stops because of high cutups, which are over $1/3$ for most pipes) but it adds great strength to the plenum and tells you, "This is the *Great*."

Charles Fisk to J. L. Coignet, July 11, 1980

My hope is to build an organ that does so well what it is supposed to do that you will not even think about what it isn't supposed to do. That is what Silbermann succeeded in doing.

Charles Fisk to Marilyn Mason, January 22, 1980

[Concerning the re-issue of Anton Heiller's Harvard recording]

Heiller's European recordings were always rather "antiseptic." The flow of musical line was not apparent on them. I agree that David Griesinger managed to take Heiller's mind *off* the machine-aspect of both the organ and the recording equipment—the result was really quite musical.

You remark that I might think a newer organ than Harvard would represent me better. But you must remember, each organ that I work on is like one of my children—I know the faults of each one, but basically love them all. I would be delighted to have Harvard on a German label. After all, I can never be sure that the organs we build now are *musically* any better than the ones we built ten or even twenty years ago.

Charles Fisk to Uwe Pape, August 1, 1982

[In reply to an inquiry on the use of zinc for organ pipes]

You may well ask why we are pleased to hear the metallic vibrations in small tin pipes, but not pleased to hear the metallic vibrations in small zinc pipes. After all, the two metals are similar in many ways. I have no good answer for this question, except to say that tin seems pleasanter than zinc no matter *how* you look at it! Bending a piece of aged zinc produces a crackling sound that is somehow unpleasant, while bending a piece of tin produces a crackling sound that is somehow pleasant. Why do we react this way? I do not know.

Charles Fisk to Alfred Reichling, August 24, 1982

I have never once forgotten that it was you and your congregation there in Lawrence that gave us our first chance to build the *new* kind of organ—the *tracker* organ, in which the player himself opens the valve that makes the pipe speak. I have been back to Redeemer Lutheran Church a number of times, and the organ still sounds good to me. Yes, the action of the organ was new-fangled then, but of course it was the very same action that Bach knew, and that Martin Luther knew. In almost a quarter of a century since Redeemer Lutheran's organ was built there has been a total reversal among U.S. organists. Most of them prefer tracker action now. But many truths have a way of starting out small, don't they! I hope that you can enjoy your part in being in on the beginning of an element of truth that Bach knew and that Luther knew, but that our civilization had unwisely forgotten. Do let the people at Downtown United Presbyterian Church [in Rochester] know that without you their organ might have been quite different!

Charles Fisk to Rev. Fredrik Nissen, February 7, 1983

An organ builder dreams of making organs so irresistible that they entrap the poor souls that play and listen to them. If Chris [Didier] becomes the organist I know you can make him, I will feel a most unusual measure of fulfillment.

Charles Fisk to David Craighead, March 11, 1983

The [Silbermann] organ I had the most time with was Grosshartmannsdorf. They will tell you this is not such an interesting organ, but I disagree. The tremulant is (or was) superb and makes the Oberwerk sound like little people from the Black Forest. I have tried copying the tremulant in this organ but without success. If you discover the secret, let me know.

The wind systems are excellent, in my opinion, and the details should be noted carefully. . . .

There is middle-European magic in the best of these organs. They make the garish ceiling paintings and organ decorations come to life. But I think you have to *improvise* when you play on them. "Real" written-down music doesn't mean much.

Charles Fisk to Jürgen Ahrend, September 15, 1983

Excerpts from the European Notebooks

[Editor's note: The following excerpts are largely from two notebooks kept by Charles Fisk. The first dates from his first trip to Europe in 1959 and contains, for the most part, stoplists, scales, and drawings. The Marmoutier instrument, one which had a profound influence on him, is the only one accorded a detailed description; this and the two shorter commentaries on Dutch organs which follow it are from the 1959 notebook. The second notebook accompanied Charles Fisk on two later trips, in 1974 and 1977, when he was investigating the work of Gottfried Silbermann and studying organs containing Gothic and Renaissance material in preparation for his work in Wellesley College. While some entries are dated (all East German entries are from 1974) many are not, and some of the North European organs have entries from both years. The final few entries, on central German organs of the Bach era, are excerpted from a "notebook" of a different sort, a tape made on a minicassette recorder which Charles Fisk took with him on a brief trip in January of 1982.]

[Abbey Church, Marmoutier, Alsace: Andreas Silbermann organ]

Impressions of Marmoutier: Fine case of oak, unpainted, good hardware. Manual keys of reversed color, very short naturals, 4″ spacing. Stops of R[ück] P[ositive] draw from back of R.P. case. Typical Silbermann case construction much like north Germans: very shallow, completely enclosed, Great in 2 chests with stop controls between chests; chests are laid out according to front pipe pattern, which usually has small tower in center, large towers at sides. Positif imitates Great. At Marmoutier, both RP and Gt. have sloping roofs over the "flat" sections, such that the sound is reversed to the rear. Possibly so that Trumpet can be accommodated on back of chest, but there seems to be plenty of room. Solid oak panelling everywhere seems to help bass resonances. Cases are moderately ornate, but in excellent taste.

Action completely simple, using backfalls a *yard* long where necessary, feel of backfalls is not bad, probably because of 1:2 reduction in stroke at key. Keys all hang from pallets. Only one coupler (RP-Gt.)

Pallet boxes are literally as small as possible, Gt. pallets are reversed from the usual and are at front of chest. They operate in normal way, using pulpits. Pallets are guided at sides by pins, glued in. They have only leather, no felt, but probably are quiet because of 1:2 reduction. Rollerboard arms are all of equal length. Keyfall on Gt. is ½″. Pallet openings always 8 ¼″ long. . . . Wind enters both Gt. chests from a common duct, between the chests in the middle. The wind for the Rp. comes in two conductors (parallel) which (appear to) run down from the Great pallet boxes and under the floor. The wind used to be raised from a bellows stack directly behind the pedal organ on a platform. At present there is a large bellows of many folds located behind the pedal. . . .

Pipework: All pipes have closed toeholes except where full wind is required. Principals are made with 80% [tin] bodies and lead feet. Languids thin and with *fairly* steep face. Silbermann used open windways, healthy cutups and apparently never more than 3 to 5 small nicks. Languids are set well into pipes, and flatting is somewhat like dubbing in; vertical scribe marks are made on inside, both in bodies and in feet. The cutup is often ¼ but occasionally more, especially for small scaled pipes in mixture. The cutup is almost never perfectly straight across; rather it is always just slightly arched. There is no skiving anywhere, but pipe walls are thin, because they are made of tin. Windways are always moderately open. The sound of the principals is always rather quiet, with a small chiff of no particular tone, followed quickly by the sound of the pipe itself. Front pipes, which nearly always have overlength, speak very well. They have round openings in the back. . . .

It is impossible to detect the presence of any facing off of the languid edge, as Stinkens does it. Principal mouths are always a full quarter of circumference. At Marmoutier the open [diapason] is of good scale. . . . Marmoutier dates from 1710 and uses smaller scales than Ebersmunster, which was by Johann Andreas Silbermann and uses fairly large scales. Muhleisen likes Marmoutier better than Ebersmunster. The characteristic of the principal chorus is that it is not at all overdone, nothing terribly loud. The flutes are of simple construction. Bourdons are always made with chimneys, which are about ¼ [of diameter] and are long. Cutups for Bourdons are ½; there is no nicking, languids are thin and with a moderately steep face. It appears that the languids are graded off toward the back, so that the back is not as thick as the front.

Generally the *types* of pipework used are few. The handling at the mouth is always the same. The Bourdons appear to use a ²⁄₉ or a ¼ mouth.

The mutations are always Flutes and are always cylindrical. They have ⅕ mouths and relatively low cutups, and are fat.

Mixtures are narrow in scale but perhaps not *quite* as narrow as in a Schnitger organ. They are full blown, having what appear to be the only open toe holes in the organ. There is still regulation on the toe.

[Alkmaar, Holland: Arp Schnitger organ]

Action stiff and rubbery. Green house over console. Schnitger pipework is like Zwolle. Even RP is voiced very loud. Mixtures hurt when you stand over them. All open toes. Mixture cut up ⅓, small scale, full blown. Upper lips are skived in a funny way. No nicks in small pipes. No chiff. Metal of lower lip is very thin, much thinner than we usually make. Schnitger used many reeds with wood burners [i.e., "doppelkegel" resonators]. Always the blocks are wooden. Shallots are brass, very wide, covered with leather in the bass. Reed sounds not very distinguished. No 8′ Trumpet on Great, but 16′ and 4′. Only Pedal 16′ is Prestant. Within the case there is no tendency *whatever* to make boxes, in fact there is room for twice as much organ within the case. The Rp. case is also much larger than necessary. The chests always follow the disposition of the front pipes. Case is not very deep.

[Beverwijk, Holland: Christian Muller organ]

This organ built in standard way, very thin, Gt. chest 2 sections. Pedal chests close to floor at either side, very direct action for pedals. Mechanical action very hard. Open toe holes throughout. Some nicking, especially 8′ stops. . . . No chiff anywhere. 16′ Fagott on Ped. is a Dulzian. . . . Big wide, open shallots.

[Frederiksborg Castle, Hillerød, Denmark: Compenius Organ]

The little 4′ Regal goes perfectly with the quintadena 8′ to produce *imitatio violinistica*.
Jungfrau Regal 4′ on Pedal very pungent, a good solo for 2 voices.
Bagpipe on F triad (4 pipes) can be alternated with manuals. You can play it in many interesting ways.
Sweelinck variations: "Soll Es Sein"
Think of the grotesque faces on the cases:
The various sounds from individual notes of the regal are like the faces! And the purpose of the faces [is] to give contrast to the beautiful things, thus to enhance the overall beauty.
Dulcian 8′ in Pedal—quiet, evocative.
An organ composed of only these reeds and some flutes is all you need for this piece.

Harald talks of "Lieblichkeit" meaning "elegance." That is what this organ has *above all*. It represents the natural reaction to the leaden pipework of the middle ages.

[Parish Church, Houdan, France: Clicquot organ]

Plein jeux's both quite bright but not tingly—foundations *mild*. Gentle but not powerless by any means. Suave sound but thin. Trumpet not especially loud (*some notes are). Cromhorne quite big sounding. Both definitely say "anche" in a way ours don't.
Thin sound, quick.
Trebles of the flue stops are fairly powerful, whether this is due to the original regulation one can't tell.
The whole sound is especially clear despite reverberant acoustics.
"Tierce jeu" is gentle, not powerful in bass.
Foundations are generally reminiscent of early American organs in output. Gentle, gentile, delicate.
Vox Humana very strong and buzzy with "anche" sound. Very sandy.
Tremulant Fort very fast, like voice vibrato.
Cornet strongly aids treble of Grand Jeu.
Reeds don't take over the bass.
Tremblant doux reasonable rate, pretty.
Principals have tin bodies, lead feet.
Recit Trumpet foundational, rather quick.
All reeds are such that a small depressing of the key brings on the speech.
Reed scales not large . . . except that Cromhorne was large in treble.
Cornets are very beautiful. Great V is a bit fuller sounding than the Recit V but level is about the same. Can't tell why these sound so nice.
Flutes very gentle, very beautiful. 8′ Prestant of G. O. is just a Dulciana, *nothing* more. The whole balance of the organ depends on holding these pipes back. 4′ prestant of G. O. is likewise light. Also 2′. Sound of mixtures however is fairly strong inside case. Cutups low for all principals. Scales seem normal for a small instrument.

[Temple de Saint Esprit, Paris: Cavaillé-Coll organ]

Bourdon is quite heavy for the manuals but is excellent. This organ was probably built after Cavaillé-Coll's death. *Very* well placed. Large Swell box with *opposed* shutters, small, working in opposite directions. (I thought I invented this!)
Beautiful tin front pipes, Roman mouths, projecting, somewhat less than ¼ mouths and without ears but with pieces of the upper lip still left at the sides of the mouths. Scale not excessive. A great deal of tin in this organ, viz., harmonic flutes, Gambas, both reeds.
This is a fantastically good instrument in a resonant building of irregular octa-

gon shape. The blending of all voices is superb, e.g., the passing from flute to string to oboe to trumpet is suave. All registers ascend markedly in the treble ... and just float in the middle and low registers. Harmonic flutes are huge; the double-length portion is actually of moderate diapason scale, moderate and normal nicking, moderate languid thickness and angles. Cutups nothing high. The Gamba is an excellent stop, though nothing we have not heard before. It has the typical C-C brass beards soldered to the sides. Nicking normal, skived upper lips, upper lips cut in Dom Bedos style but totally flat the length of the scribed lines. . . . Reeds look very typical, thin tin, shallots sort of square ended (but domed), tongues absolutely square ended. These reeds are perfect. They are quick, even, in tune, not very overpowering, but not at all shrinking. . . .

[Langwarden, Germany]

Prestant 4': Dark quality of pure lead. Not so Lieblich or elegant; there's a sweet roughness.
8' Ged., 4' & 2' are almost like a mixture because they push so hard. . . .
8' Brustwerk flute of wood *very* Lieblich, gentle, elegant.
4' Open flute, Brustwerk: narrow, lieblich, a bit like King's Chapel.
2' BW is very scharf . . .
8' Discant Schweitzerpfeife is very narrow, sounds like traverso. Metal stop.
4' Spitzflöte Gt. is very narrow, lieblich, reminds us of 4' at Huntington, Swell.
8' Quintadena & Gedeckt together are lieblich.
8 + 4 + 2 ⅔ + 2 is very mixture-like.
This organ is important because it combines the lead [pipework] with later ideas. It is the missing link between Fritzsche and Schnitger.
Pedal 1' stop (flute) works well with 2' cornet. It's very interesting to me that there were situations in Germany where a big organ could overpower the *Leute* the way our organs sometimes do.

[St. Cosmae Church, Stade, Germany: Schnitger organ]

The wind in Stade is exceptionally stable for an old organ. Jürgen Ahrend says he reconstructed the wind system as well as he could. Of special interest is the bifurcation for the Great chests! Apparently it was standard to come up with a largish duct, perhaps 4" x 10" section, and connect to the chests with short ducts of much smaller section, perhaps 4" x 4". I wonder if the small short length of duct acts mainly as a *resistance* rather than an inductance or capacitance. We must try narrowing the openings into our chests as a way of avoiding unwanted vibrations in the wind.

[Oosthuizen, Holland: Gothic organ]

Prestant 8′ seems to be only register straight through by original builders. Tops have been added to a good deal. Tuned by tongues of metal. Best pipe is middle C which has been protected inside organ. Many pipes don't get enough wind.
Bourdon—originally 8′, has been lengthened to 16′. If originally scale it now is, it was huge.
Woudfluit is fat and contributes greatly to characteristic sound of the organ (Dutch). Pipework is frightfully battered, but enough good pipes remain to show what it once must have sounded like.
Nothing is held back, but the foundations speak very gently, perhaps due to less winding from the chest.

General characteristic of the sound is that of small scale, heavy wall lead pipes with thin languids having the bjeezus blown out of them. Chiff is avoided by rough languid-&-lower-lip and by some nicking, also gegenphase. Few pipes of the lower register are without gegenphase. The lower and upper lips never look like those of a new pipe. They are not usually skived, but on the other hand there is usually some blunting, something that eliminates sharp, machined edges. Maybe the same knife that produced the gegenphase was used to round the inner edge of the lower lip. Often there is a burr on the outer corner (arras) of the lower lip, as though caused by burnishing. Because of gegenphase, most languids have to be banged down considerably. Speech is often hesitant but without chiff. The characteristic of the full sound is bright and fierce (brave) but without any of Silbermann's scratch.

[Steinkirchen, Germany: Schnitger organ]

A very cold church; a very beautiful organ. The Prestant 8′ by Schnitger is very lovely, better than I had remembered. It uses Schnitger's standard material, i.e. 20% tin. The sound is very gentle but solid.
The 8′ Rohrflute and 2⅔′ Nazat on the Great are very old and beautiful—from Scherer. The combination of these 2 with the tremulant . . . is very beautiful indeed—the heart of this instrument. The Rohrflute is heavy lead but better made than usual, with cleaner than usual languids, soldered-on caps,

big tuning ears, short, rather small rohrs. It is definitely a stop worth repeating.... The Nazard is a huge tapered stop. Wind trunks are of course very small and therefore the response to the tremolo is very natural. Like Silbermann the main Gt. windtrunk divides in two just before entering the Gt. chests.
The 8′ Krumphorn [sic] on the Bw is very good.... H[arald Vogel] says the resonators are Schnitger but the shallots are older. The sound is mild throughout compass, slightly bee-in-a-bottle-y. It is close to the sound of an actual Krumhorn.

[Osterholz-Scharmbeck, Germany: Bielefeld organ]

The best stop in the organ is the 8′ Spitzflöte on the Great, a highly tapered stop that sings very nicely. Next best is the Posaune 16′ on the Pedal, with its original tongues yet. Both are quite Schnitgerish. As in all Schnitger organs the foundations are mild, especially Ped. 8′ and 4′ which work extremely well in trios. Even without nicking there is no chiff to these pipes—they simply go to their note easily. The tremulant is very good, of the Schnitger type outside the wind trunk. Wind system is made new to the old measurements and seems quite satisfactory. Bellows, however, is rectangular, which seems to make no real difficulties. I was interested to see that the tremolo is reasonably close to the bellows, unlike the one at Steinkirchen. Actual position may not make the difference.

[Krewerd (Province Groningen), Holland: Renaissance organ]

An incredible renaissance instrument of few stops but great power. The little Gothic church intensifies the sound, but even so the soaring quality of the chorus 8–4–2 ⅔′(?)–2′ is unbelievable. This was the most "vocale" sound I heard and is doubtless the best model for a Sweelinck organ.
The [pipe] metal is the usual old heavy lead, hammered and battered.
[On a later visit:] Again an unbelievable sound. Got to look at interior this time. Cutups huge but pipes don't seem terribly unusual, except that the windways are huge. The boldness is incredible.

[St. George's Church, Rötha, Germany: Gottfried Silbermann organ]

A typical 2 manual organ of Gottfried Silbermann.... the striking thing is that there are no manual reeds, but the pedal has 16′, 16′ & 8′, of which last 2 are reeds. Originally no pedal coupler—one has been applied more recently. Pedal reeds—very French. Trumpet—large tin resonators [like] French ones with small tips. . . . Different from French in that these [have] wooden blocks and boots—typically German.

16′ Posaune. Nicely made wooden resonators. Having seen Dave's slides not surprised at shallots which are French but made with heavy lead instead of brass. . . . Nice plump sound [like] German reeds but more pizazz.

16′ Open—of wood, what kind? Nicely made. Moderate scale [like] Center Church. Blocks are beveled but the caps are hollow too & caps set slightly below blocks. Speaks very well. Puts out a lot of fundamental—seems on a larger scale & sounds rather French.

Principal all in tin—feet and all. Looks just like A. Silbermann even scaling of upperwork—slender in the bass and less slender in the treble. Uses gerissen mouths (a la Dom Bedos). This flatting does cause a buck-tooth effect, makes it very easy to voice.

Sound of pipework: all of it pushed (or free?) Amazing that an organ so old can really scratch, not cut back at all. A large sound, the ensemble has a throaty or sensual sound. Quality of pushed sound in every register. No effort made to cut back basses or upperwork. Mutations all strong all the way down. Congeal very well—the whole organ hangs together very well.

Principals broad and not screechy. All stops in roughly the same dynamic level & different colors in every register.

Cornet of Gr. did not work against just flutes in Ow.—have to have [principals] as well.

Amazing that an organ this good can come down virtually undisturbed.

Large, generous, colorful instrument. Offered a lot of variety.

A really singing instrument. Principal 8′ . . . very large and singing. Partially due to winding.

[Grosshartmannsdorf, Germany: Gottfried Silbermann organ]

This was [Silbermann's] 45th organ . . . completed in 1741—one of his last instruments. He must have built a number of organs like this; shows every sign of perfection of a certain kind of organ. The Great chests are separated in the middle to allow the Oberwerk action to come through & to allow the Oberwerk to come down closely over the Great chests. The wind ducts come as usual across the walkboards then divide and traverse the inside ends of the chests to reach the pallet boxes which are always on the fronts of the chests with the bungboards facing back. Everything is a model of accessibility. The tremulant is in the Great wind trunk just back of the Gt. walkboard and affects every stop in the organ, perhaps because of leaks. Its effect on the Oberwerk is unbelievably beautiful, quite strong.

The pitch of the organ is a strong half step high. Wind pressure is 3½ [inches]. Most of pipework is very full blown & the sound of full organ is almost deafening inside the case. The Oberwerk especially is full blown even in its mutations and there is no attempt at all to soften the mutations as they descend to low C. The 8′ Gedackt is stopped wood in its lowest octave but becomes a normal metal Gedackt with ears from there up. The tuning caps are leathered although one could tune using the ears. The nicking in this organ is more pronounced . . . than in Rötha and in general is much like the nicking we use. This Gedackt has no unusual characteristic but responds beautifully to the winding. The 4′ Rohrflöte looks a lot like the Gedackt. It has small rather short chimneys. The top octave is spitzflute pipes. Again I can detect no particularly unusual qualities except the unusual response to the wind.

The 2′ Octave is tin, full blown—has broad windways all the way up and down. Considerable nicking in the bass and looks just like the pipework in Rötha. The overshot upper lips are produced here by making the mouth width of the foot greater than the mouth width of the body. The toe holes are generally very large though certainly not open.

The Tertz 1⅗′ surprisingly enough is of principal scale and blown quite full. It works extremely well in both the French and German way, probably because it competes equally with all the other ranks.

I measured the sifflöte 1′ because it is identical in scale to the mixture [and] is the key to the mixture. In general all of the principal work seems to be of a piece which is why it cohabits so beautifully.

The entire Principal is in the prospect. The 2 upper flats are dummies—which scandalized G. Becker and Chas. Krigbaum. The gold of the carvings is exceptionally nice. And while the Silbermann cases always have an overplump look in the pictures, there is something very right about them in the actuality.

[*Excerpts from tape made in East Germany, January 1982*]

[Klettbach: Johann Georg Schroeter organ, 1725]

This is an organ that is within ten miles of Weimar, very close to Arnstadt. Has no reed on the manuals and has only a Posaune in the Pedal. The church is a typical small church with double decked galleries on the sides and back. The organ stands in the second gallery in the back. It is a 4-foot case with an Oberwerk in the middle and the Great 4′ standing at the sides of the Oberwerk and the action running up between the two Great chests. It's actually a very sensible use of space. The Pedal as usual is behind, the walkboard running between the Pedal Posaune and the Great chestwork.

The specification of the Great is remarkable in terms of what people think a Baroque organ ought to be, especially a Bach organ, there being no 8′ Open [Diapason]. There are, nevertheless, three 8′ stops, and they are an 8′ Gamba, which looks like any one of our Gambas in scale, except it's even smaller in the treble; also a Gemshorn 8′, about the same scale as our typical 4′ Gemshorn, such as at Harvard, Swell; and a Quintadena 8′. All of the pipework is constructed of paper-thin material. It's so thin that if you pick it up without care you'll push dents in the pipes.

All pipework is overshot in that there's a strong tendency to make the pipework with the feet too small; any ordinary pipemaker would think he'd made the feet too small. This tendency is extremely obvious in the Gamba; it's perfectly obvious that the feet are too small. There's no question in my mind that this is done to make the pipes speak better.

The pipes spoke with a very clear and gentle sound. It's perfectly clear that if you make an organ this way, with thin pipes like this, the chances are that it has a gentle silvery sound about it, far gentler than a typical Silbermann. I don't believe you can force this pipework the way Silbermann did, and certainly it's not cut up the way Silbermann did.

Chorus work is straight-line scaling, by which I mean the Twelfth and Fifteenth and Mixture are all made to the same scale stick. I would describe the scales as neither very small or very large. They seem small to Fritz [Schild] and Harald [Vogel], but they seem like normal chorus work to me. It's quite remarkable how small-scale the Gedeckts are in this organ. The Quintadena of course has box beards, on the Great, but there's a Gedeckt 8′ on the Oberwerk that's scarcely any larger than a Quintadena. The Posaune is a huge stop in scale and has tremendously thick tongues vibrating against wooden shallots. . . . They're really long, because of the thickness of the tongues—the tongues are real railroad-car springs—and nothing is leathered. The tongue just beats against the wood. It's quite a formidable sound. . . .

[Muhlberg: Volkland organ, 1729]

[This is] a larger organ than the one in Klettbach, and it's better built. It has two manuals and pedal. The same arrangement of chests as Klettbach because the ceiling is so close to the organ; that is, there's an Oberwerk in the middle up high, and then the Great is divided in two chests at either side of the organ with the 8-foot towers on either side, and then the Pedal is behind.

This organ in the Pedal has a Violone of about 5x6 inside diameter at low C, with very thin walls. . . . It breaks into oak fronts down low, that is, near the bottom of the pipe, and then has perfectly normal mouthing as nearly as we can tell. And then somebody has stuck a little piece of tracker in on an angle, between the . . . sides of the mouth, to provide a beard that no doubt does the same sort of thing that Hook used to do when they put a sliver of pipe metal sticking out at an angle from the cap of their Pedal Opens.

A curious feature of all these organs is that the Great bungboard is available only from the front of the organ. Now, this is simple of construction in a Gothic organ where everything is flat across the front, but when the pipe towers are all articulating the façade of the organ, it ends up that you have bits of tower fronts all along the front of the organ that must be just removed by hand, exposing the bungboards of the Great.

Again and again we see a sticker action on the lower manual that works the Great and goes down to a rollerboard that's directly under the Great, sort of between the Great and the Pedal, and then runs out to the sides and up to the Great.

There's a very standard shape to the cases of this area. . . .

[Schmalkalden: Meyer organ, late 16th Century]

A Renaissance castle in which there's a chapel, the whole thing from about 1589. All the design work in the place is in Renaissance style, and it has that sort of strap-work that one associates with the Compenius organ.

This is a one-manual organ in a small chapel in the castle. The chapel has three levels of balcony in it, as well as the main floor. It's a little bit like the Fogg Museum in Cambridge. Reminiscent of the chapel in Frederiksborg; reminiscent of the pictures of the chapel in Weimar where Bach played for nine years or whatever it was. The ceiling of the chapel is gently vaulted and is decorated in plaster which they polychromed in a very beautiful and airy style. The whole thing is totally free of anything that looks Baroque. They say the style, which I've always associated with the Danes, actually came from the Flemish countries. The organ stands in the top gallery, just as shown in the Weimar castle chapel. It's very close to the ceiling. . . . It sounds just gorgeous in that position. The acoustics seem to be just wonderful. One supposes the same thing was true in Weimar, especially since one guesses that the Weimar materials might have been the same sort of plaster and complicated balcony fronts.

The organ has a total of six registers: Gedeckt 8', Principal 4', Spitzflute 2', Cymbal I rank, and two reed stops. All of them are made of wood; the four flues are original. . . . The Principal is the best stop in the organ. It looks like an ordinary Grossflute, except it's got ivory coverings on it. It has beautiful long feet, decorated. One wonders what effect those might have had on it. I remember Hemmersam telling me that the trouble with ordinary wooden pipes was the way the wind had to be led around inside them, and of course he always made tapered feet on his wood pipes, like the Compenius organ front pipes.

The Cymbal is on the back row and therefore quite visible. It's quite an unusual arrangement. First of all, it's entirely little wooden pipes, and the little wooden pipes, instead of standing on toes on a toeboard . . . are glued on their backs across the toeboard. They're so short they fit that way. The pipes themselves look quite stubby, as though they would have quite a fat sound to them, but if you look at them closely you see that the walls are very thick and that the actual bore of the pipe—the air column—is really quite small in scale, meaning that the scale is probably not too different from that of a typical metal Cymbal. . . . Obviously a great deal of effort has been put into making everything just right and everything perfect so that it works evenly, and in fact it works just beautifully. . . .

The case of the organ is very, very beautiful. First of all you have these wood pipes standing in three towers, and then there are two flats, between. And the façades of these pipes are simply covered in ivory, which really gives it all kinds of class. The two side towers are v-towers, and the center pipe on each one of these is a sort of . . . Doppleflute kind of thing in which mouths are speaking in two directions at right angles to each other. It turns out that these two center pipes of the v-towers are dummies. We wondered how [the builder] got out of the problem, and that's the way he did.

The output of this organ is considerably more than the Compenius organ; a little on the boisterous side, and very nice indeed. Very beautiful sound. The fact that it's in meantone assists this effect greatly. Most boisterous of all of course is the 4' [Principal], since it stands in the front.

SEA MOSSING AT MILK ISLAND

Milk Island, milk of the sea
Goatsherd apocalypse, wading out to me.
Thrust to thine hands, O God,
Trust and thrust to thee alone
Seagull's maneuver, straws down wind,
Rockweed nest by rounded stone.

Once was boy with rake so square,
Racked against rock your seaweed hair;
Heisted high and into the hold,
Glove on rake, glove on rake,
Multiplying there the take
Of weed to make his own kill-bone.

When black wind at sunset blew,
Stood he then his dory to,
Leaned to sky, to old gull's cry,
Sea-harvest gleaned, his rake astrew—
And suddenly knew, and suddenly knew
It was the God-wind there that blew.

CHARLES FISK
January 1969

[Editor's note: Charles Fisk spent the summers of his childhood in Rockport, on Cape Ann, to which he later returned in adult life. As a teenager, he earned money during the summer by harvesting sea moss on the rocky islands off the Rockport shore. Milk Island was one of these, used at one time to pasture goats and other livestock during the summer months, but now inhabited only by gulls. Charles Fisk always loved the seacoast, and the powerful impression made on his youthful mind by his close and solitary contact with it on Milk Island prompted the writing of this poem many years later.]

Discography

OPUS 28: *Redeemer Lutheran Church, Lawrence, Massachusetts, 1959*
Melville Smith, "Postlude" (with three other organs). (Organ Historical Society)

OPUS 35: *Mount Calvary Church, Baltimore, Maryland, 1961*
John Fesperman, "An Organ Recital." (Cambridge Records)

OPUS 44: *King's Chapel, Boston, Massachusetts, 1964*
Joseph Payne, "Organ Masterpieces from the Fitzwilliam Virginal Book." (Vox PL 14.380)

OPUS 46: *Memorial Church, Harvard University, 1967*
E. Power Biggs, "The Organ in Sight and Sound" (Ives's *Variations* only). (Columbia KS 7263)

Arthur Carkeek, "The Charles Fisk Organs at Harvard, DePauw and West Church." (DePauw University School of Music 46135)

John Ferris and University Choir, "Dedication Service of C.B. Fisk Organ." (Sonic Press)

Martha Folts, "A Sonic Experience with Martha Folts at Harvard." (Delos Records DEL 25448)

Anton Heiller, "Heiller plays Hindemith at Harvard." (Harvard Square Records DGR 73-3)

Joan Lippincott, "Concertos by J.S. Bach." (Gothic Records)

Joan Lippincott, "Preludes and Fugues and Passacaglia by J.S. Bach." (Gothic Records)

Lawrence Moe, "Works of Georg Böhm and Johann Pachelbel." (Cambridge Records CRS 2514)

Christa Rakich, "J.S. Bach's Clavierübung, Part III." (Titanic Records Ti-91 and Ti-92)

Harvard University Choir, "Christmas in Cambridge." (David Griesinger Recordings HMC-75)

OPUS 48A: *DePauw University, Greencastle, Indiana, 1965*
Arthur Carkeek, "The Charles Fisk Organs at Harvard, DePauw and West Church." (DePauw University School of Music 46135)

OPUS 55: *Old West Church, Boston, Massachusetts, 1971*
E. Power Biggs, "The Stars and Stripes Forever" (with two other organs). (Columbia M 34129)

Arthur Carkeek, "The Charles Fisk Organs at Harvard, DePauw, and West Church." (DePauw University School of Music 46135)

John Fesperman, "John Fesperman playing the Fisk Organ in the West Church." (Cambridge Records 2504)

Brian Jones, "A Boston Organ Tour" (with two other organs). (AFKA Records)

Mireille Lagacé, "Dietrich Buxtehude." (Titanic Records Ti-11)

Max Miller, "Felix Mendelssohn-Bartholdy's Grand Ensemble for Organ." (Musical Heritage Society MHS 3731)

Frank Taylor, "DuMage and D'Andrieu." (Elysée Editions SD 1001)

Frank Taylor, "Louis Marchand, The Complete Organ Works." (Elysée Editions SDA 1005/6)

OPUS 68: *University of Vermont, Burlington, Vermont, 1976*
John Fesperman, "Nicolas de Grigny." (Orion ORS 76253)

OPUS 72: *Houghton Chapel, Wellesley College, 1981*
Lynn Edwards and Edward Pepe, works of Bach, Böhm, Reincken and Buxtehude (Westfield Center cassette)

Frances Fitch and les Filles de Sainte-Colombe, "Seventeenth Century English Music for Viols and Organ." (Titanic Ti-95)

Harald Vogel, "The Fisk Organ at Wellesley College: A Revival of the Meantone Tradition." (Organa 3005)

Harald Vogel, works of Böhm, Buxtehude, Kuhnau and Bach. (Westfield Center cassette)

OPUS 78: *House of Hope Presbyterian Church, St. Paul, Minnesota, 1979*
Nancy Lancaster, "Music from House of Hope Presbyterian Church." (House of Hope Record No. HOH 101)

Joan Lippincott, "Toccatas and Fugues by Bach." (Gothic Records 68005)

Joan Lippincott, "Fantasia and Fugue on Ad Nos, Ad Salutarem Undam" and "Grand Pièce Symphonique." (Gothic Records 98212)

Joan Lippincott, "Epiphanies—Revelations—Man's Days are like the Grass." (Gothic Records 18313)

OPUS 83: *Downtown United Presbyterian Church, Rochester, New York, 1983*
J. Melvin Butler, "Organ Music from Downtown Presbyterian Church." (Downtown Presbyterian Church)

H. Joseph Butler, "André Raison: A Study in French Organ Liturgy." (Pro Organo 7008; cassette)

Barbara Harbach and the Rochester Singers, "American Hymn Preludes." (Gasparo #GS258)

OPUS 84: *Abbey Chapel, Mount Holyoke College, South Hadley, Massachusetts 1984*
Margaret Irwin-Brandon, (Music of Bach; in preparation)

OPUS 85: *Memorial Church, Stanford University, 1984*
Robert Bates, (in preparation)

Sandra Soderlund, Two demonstration cassettes.

Harald Vogel, "The Stanford Organ." (Organa 3008)

OPUS 86: *St. Matthew's Church, Pacific Palisades, California, 1985*
David Britton, (Music of Bach; in preparation)

Bibliography

Bermar, Amy. "C. B. Fisk: Organ Maker," *Gloucester Magazine*, Vol. IV No. 1 (Winter 1981).

Bichel, Daryl. "The Charles Fisk Organ at Old West Church," *Old West Organ Society Journal*, Vol. 1 No. 1 (1984).

Boykin, John. "Building 'em Like They Used To," *The Stanford Magazine*, Vol. 12 No. 1 (Spring 1984).

Bozeman, George, Jr. "C. B. Fisk, Inc. of Gloucester, Massachusetts," *Art of the Organ*, Vol. 1 No. 1 (Dec. 1971).

Brown, Ned. "Making Organs Speak," *North Shore*, April 6, 1968.

"Center Church, New Haven, Has New Fisk Organ," *The Diapason*, Vol. 64 No. 1 (Dec. 1972).

"Charles Fisk's Kingly Instrument," *Harvard Alumni Bulletin*, Vol. 70 No. 8 (Feb. 3, 1968).

"Charles Fisk, 58, Builder of Organs" (Obituary), *Gloucester Daily Times*, Dec. 19, 1983.

"Charles B. Fisk, at 58, renowned organ builder" (Obituary), *The Boston Globe*, Jan. 11, 1984.

"Christ Episcopal Church, Westerly, R.I." *The American Organist*, Vol. 49 No. 4 (Apr. 1966).

"Christ United Methodist Church, Greensboro, North Carolina," *The American Organist*, Vol. 17 No. 10 (Oct. 1984).

Coffey, Mark D. *Charles Fisk: Organ Builder*, Eastman School of Music D. M. A. Dissertation, 1984.

Cornell, Robert. "The Fisk Organ at Mount Holyoke College," *Early Keyboard Studies Newsletter*, Vol. 1 No. 2 (March 1985).

Cornell, Robert. "Stanford: A Rare Opportunity for Organ Building," *The Diapason*, Vol. 75 No. 6 (June 1984).

Decenzo, John. "Rockporters Work on $100,000 Organ for Harvard Church," *Gloucester Times*, Jan. 4, 1967.

"Downtown Presbyterian Church, Rochester, New York," *The American Organist*, Vol. 18 No. 1 (Jan. 1985).

Dyer, Richard. "Historic Box of Whistles," *Boston Sunday Globe*, Sept. 27, 1981.

Fesperman, John. "The Fisk Organ in Old West Church, Boston, U.S.A.," *The Organ Yearbook*, 1974.

Fesperman, John. *Two Essays on Organ Design* (Raleigh: The Sunbury Press, 1975).

"Fisk Tracker Organ Being Erected at Christ Church," *Westerly Sun*, Feb. 14, 1965.

"Fisk to Build Tracker for Harvard Memorial," *The Diapason*, Vol. 55 No. 1 (Dec. 1963).

Flint, Edward W. "The C. B. Fisk Organ at Harvard University," *The Organ*, Vol. 48 No. 190 (1968).

Folts, Martha. "House of Hope Organ Institute," *The Diapason*, Vol. 74 No. 12 (Dec. 1983).

"Former student builds a baroque organ," *Stanford Observer*, 1982.

Frank, Gerald. "The Organ and the Concert Hall," *The American Organist*, Vol. 16 No. 3 (March 1982).

Garland, Joe. "Organ Pipes fashioned of wood are cabinetmaker's specialty," *North Shore*, May 20, 1972.

Gomes, Peter J. "Charles Fisk, 1925–1983," *The American Organist*, Vol. 18 No. 3 (March 1984).

Hamilton, John. "An Emerging US Organ-Building Movement," *The Musical Times*, (June and July 1984).

Heslin, Alice Mae. "Over 400 view new Fisk organ," *The Rockport Eagle*, Feb. 12, 1970.

Hill, Cynthia. "New Organ is a master's legacy," *Palo Alto Weekly*, June 27, 1984.

Irving, Margaret. "Their skilled fingers fashion the Instrument of Bach," *Gloucester Daily Times*, Mar. 4, 1964.

Jander, Owen. "A Unique Historical Pipe Organ for Wellesley College," *Wellesley Magazine*, Vol. 62 No. 1 (Fall 1977).

Jander, Owen. "Charles Fisk's Opus 72 for Wellesley College," *L'Orgue a nôtre époque* (Montreal, McGill University, 1981).

Jander, Owen. "The Wellesley Organ's 'Breath of Life' As It Affects the Music of Buxtehude," *Charles Brenton Fisk, Organ Builder* (Easthampton: The Westfield Center for Early Keyboard Studies, 1986).

Kenyon, Nicholas. "One Perfect Harmony," *The New Yorker* (July 6, 1981).

"King's Chapel, Boston, Mass.," *The American Organist*, Vol. 47 No. 9 (Sept. 1964).

Lawrence, Arthur. "The New Fisk Organ in St. Paul," *The Diapason*, Vol. 71 No. 2 (Feb. 1980).

Martin, D. R. "The Sensual Pipe Organ," *Minnesota Monthly*, (Feb. 1980).

Mauro, Tony. "Fisk Organs built slowly but well," *Gloucester Daily Times*, Oct. 12, 1974.

Mouat, Lucia. "Debut at King's Chapel," *The Christian Science Monitor*, Feb. 1, 1964.

Mowers, Culver. "Fisk in Cazenovia," *The Tracker*, Vol. 22 No. 1 (Fall 1977).

Muckle, Kathy. "Central Christian Gets New Organ," *Huntington Herald-Press*, July 11, 1976.

"New Fisk Organ in Boston's Old West Church," *The Diapason*, Vol. 62 No. 12 (Dec. 1971).

Ochse, Orpha. *The History of the Organ in the United States* (Bloomington: Indiana University Press, 1975).

"Organ Festival, Mount Calvary Church," *Organ Institute Quarterly*, Vol. 9 No. 3 (Special Issue, 1961).

O'Toole, Elizabeth. "Cape Ann Craftsmen," *The Rockport Eagle*, Feb. 25, 1971.

Owen, Barbara. "Charles Fisk," *Grove's Dictionary Instrument Supplement* (London, 1985).

Owen, Barbara. "Meantone Temperament: A 'New' Horizon," *The Diapason*, Vol. 73 No. 11 (Nov. 1982).

Owen, Barbara. "Organists' Holiday at Storrs," *The American Organist*, Vol. 16 No. 3 (March 1982).

Owen, Barbara. *The Organs and Music of King's Chapel* (Boston: King's Chapel, 1966).

Panetta, Jay. "Harald Vogel at Wellesley: The Meantone Temperament Seminar," *The American Organist*, Vol. 17 No. 3 (March 1983).

Pape, Uwe. *The Tracker Organ Revival in America* (Berlin: Pape Verlag, 1978).

Pape, Uwe, ed. *Organs in America*, Vol. 1 (Berlin: Pape Verlag, 1982).

Porter, William. "The New Fisk Organ at Wellesley College," *The Diapason*, Vol. 73 No. 2 (Feb. 1982).

Reich, Robert J. "The Organ at the First Religious Society, Newburyport," *The Tracker*, Vol. 2 No. 1 (Oct. 1957).

Salisbury, Wilma. "Wiggly Wind Blows no Ill for Organ Maker," *Cleveland Plain Dealer*, Dec. 12, 1970.

Seagrave, Sterling. "Physicist Quits Science to Construct an Organ Like One Bach used to Play," *Baltimore American*, May 7, 1961.

Sedgwick, John. "Charles Fisk, Organ Builder," *Technology Illustrated*, Vol. 3 No. 2 (Feb. 1983).

Sedgwick, John. "Organ Builder restores principles of a vanished age," *Lawrence Eagle-Tribune*, Mar. 17, 1983.

Sly, Allan. "Church Organ Dedicated," *Westerly Sun*, June 14, 1965.

Stevens, Bruce. "House of Hope Organ Conference," *The Diapason*, Vol. 73 No. 2 (Feb. 1982).

Taylor, Frank. "The New Fisk Organ at the University of Vermont—A Review," *The Diapason*, Vol. 67 No. 8 (July 1976).

Van Tuyl, Laura. "Chapel acquires Organ," *Mount Holyoke News*, Feb. 24, 1984.

Wasserman, Jim. "Box of Whistles home in Church," *Fort Wayne Journal-Gazette*, July 27, 1976.

Walker, Ruth. "Wellesley builds new 'old' Organ," *Christian Science Monitor*, Sept. 10, 1974.

Walsh, Rosanne. "St. Paul's to dedicate new Alleluia Organ," *Willimantic Chronicle*, Jan. 4, 1975.

Welch, James. "The Organs of Memorial Church, Stanford University," *The American Organist*, Vol. 18 No. 4 (April 1984).

Yocum, Keith R. "Charles Fisk, Organ Builder," *Country Journal*, Dec. 1979.

One thousand copies of the two-volume CHARLES BRENTON FISK, ORGAN BUILDER books were designed by Carol J. Blinn of Warwick Press, Easthampton, Massachusetts. The Studley Press of Dalton, Massachusetts, set the books in W. A. Dwiggins's Electra typeface and printed them on Mohawk Superfine Softwhite. The binding with Commodore Natuurlinnen Dutch cloth was done by General Bookbinding Company, Agawam, Massachusetts. Claudia Cohen of Easthampton, Massachusetts hand made the traycases for the deluxe copies.